ALL FOR JESUS

Stanley Barnes MA

AMBASSADOR
Belfast • Greenville

All For Jesus
© 1996 Stanley Barnes MA

First published 1996

ISBN 1 898787 83 2

AMBASSADOR PRODUCTIONS LTD,
Providence House
16 Hillview Avenue,
Belfast, BT5 6JR
Northern Ireland

Emerald House,
1 Chick Springs Road, Suite 206
Greenville,
South Carolina 29609
United States of America

CONTENTS

FOREWORD

By Ian R. K. Paisley, DD, MP, MEP

"NICHOL - SON?" "AYE, BUT 18 CARAT GOLD!"

Wm. P Nicholson is a name to conjure with in the sphere of Ulster's religious life.

He occupies a place entirely by himself.

To say he was unique is to be guilty of colossal understatement.

There is no doubt God has His man for the hour and His hour for the man, and when He fashions that man He breaks the mould.

In the midst of civil war in Northern Ireland, resulting from the Irish Republican attempt to sever our Province from the United Kingdom, Wm. P Nicholson, a Presbyterian minister and a Bangorian by birth, arrived in Ulster from the United States of America preaching the Gospel.

He preached in the language of the working classes and, like His Master, the common people heard him gladly. So plain was his speech his critics called him the *"Vulgar Evangelist"*.

He had, however, the cutting edge of the Spirit's almighty anointing and the walls of the Ulster Jericho toppled before the blasts of his ram's horn Gospel Trumpet.

"From Civil War To Revival Victory" best sums up the harvest of his evangelistic exploits.

His was a ministry stamped with fearlessness and faithfulness and many rose up to call him blessed.

Principal John Barkley, a bitter opponent of all Nicholson stood for, in his history *"St Enoch's Congregation 1872-1972"* states:
"These figures show that the greatest impact on the spiritual life of the congregation was made by WP Nicholson. The increase in the number of communicants and the number of new communicants in 1923-24 make this clear. Further, it should be noted that the increased number was maintained for about seven years although this may have been partly due to the influence of later missions. On the other hand, there was no increase in congregational membership."

This testimony to the permanent result of Mr Nicholson's ministry from one of his detractors is a striking fulfilment of the Scripture precept, *"our enemies themselves being judges"*.

Every effort to help record his ministry for those who did not live in his generation is to be welcomed.

It is to be greatly regretted that because of his second wife's orders an embargo was placed on access to his original papers and thus the production of a definitive biography.

My friend and colleague, Mr Barnes, is to be congratulated on the work he has done and I believe his book will be a valuable addition to what, alas, is a very limited treasury of Nicholson memorabilia.

May the story of Wm. P Nicholson stir us all up to seek God for such a revival in our day as was so greatly manifested in his.

Chapter One

WHO WAS WILLIAM PATTESON NICHOLSON?

Even today there is much controversy over William Nicholson. Not everyone would agree as to their assessment of the man and his ministry. Some still laugh as they recall stories about his unique sense of Ulster humour both in and out of the pulpit, but others abhorred his language which was at times rude and vulgar and ungracious as he indulged in personal abuse of not only those who had dared to criticise him but also of anyone who may have interrupted the meetings by late arrival or early departure. The Rev. John Pollock, minister of St. Enoch's Presbyterian Church commented, "Some of the things he says sound bad when read in cold type, but they 'taste good' when accompanied by his genial smile which sometimes breaks into a loud and most infectious guffaw. He is a genuine humorist and knows well how to substantiate the saying 'he who laughs is not far from tears.' I have seen his vast audiences convulsed with laughter, and cheering uproariously and within ten seconds sitting in solemn stillness under the spell of his pathos."

Some looked on William Nicholson as their spiritual Joshua under whose ministry they received the blessing of the fullness of the Holy Spirit. But he ministered to sinners as well as to saints; thousands around the world look back with thankfulness to Almighty God that under Nicholson's evangelistic ministry they entered into a saving relationship with Christ. The gospel W. P. Nicholson preached was one of repentance and faith. No allowance was made for a middle course or any compromise. As the Puritans have said, "It is either turn or burn." Straight preaching of that kind produced genuine converts. Many found fault with his blunt manner, but were later forced to acknowledge that the preaching which causes men to make restitution of stolen property and others to pay long-standing debts must be preaching of the genuine kind.

Others call attention to the period after the early 1920s when some of the churches closed their pulpits to him because of his attacks upon modernists and liberals of the main denominations. These modernists and liberals questioned the authority of the Bible as the inspired Word of God. He often said in his preaching that "he believed the Bible from cover to cover." This fervent belief compelled Nicholson to fiercely condemn all who attacked the deity of Christ and the saving power of Christ's atoning blood.

Still others speak of the positive and lasting results of his missions. The local minister of the Presbyterian Church in Newtownards, describing the results of the mission held there in 1921 said:

It is sufficient testimony to the widespread feeling which prevails in the town to say that ministers are being stopped in the street by people who are anxious about their relationship to God, and that daily the homes of well-known Christian workers are being sought out by old and young, that they may learn the way of life.

One of the most outstanding features of Nicholson's ministry is the number of men in mid-life who stood and openly confessed their willingness to accept Christ during the appeals he often made in his "men only" meetings. Never has any evangelist seen such a marked and definite movement among men bordering on or over fifty years of age. This in itself is a testimony to the stability, strength and depth of his work. Often a supercilious and short-sighted judgement wags its head and says, regarding evangelistic work, "It is the usual turn for old women and children." Nobody can say that of the present movement in our town. The work began amongst the men, and is largely carried out by men.

It was after one of the later missions held in Ballymacarrett in 1923 that the Rev. John Redmond spoke of open-air work being started in the district and said, "We have already had thirty conversions, mostly of men—some of whom were gunmen during the riots."

Dr. James Dunlop said, "I have never known one who under God, made such an appeal to men particularly in their own language."

The Nicholson missions resulted in the conversion of men by the thousands. Belfast Shipyard workers marched in their hundreds from their work to churches in the city wherever the United Missions were taking place.

It is the opinion of many that the Nicholson missions which took place in the early Twenties when "murder and destruction for the time being seemed to be on the throne," had the effect of transforming the situation from civil war to revival victory.

A Roman Catholic from the Falls Road area of the city said words to the effect, "there must be something in the preaching of this man, because fellows who were trying to shoot him were now trying to convert him." Dr. T. M. Johnston, a Moderator of the General Assembly, in his biography says, "But this I say for a certainty, that more lasting good was done to our Province during the Nicholson mission than by any other in my time."

Who was W. P. Nicholson? The question still has not been fully answered. Why has no major biography been written about him? What about his background? What about his wider ministry outside his own country? As he travelled the world twelve times preaching the gospel, what were the secrets of his success as an evangelist? These and many other questions still remain to be answered.

It is not the purpose of this present writer to defend William Patteson Nicholson in all that he said, did or believed. However, together we will hopefully have a better understanding of the man and his message, and we will follow him even as he followed Christ.

The reader is left to make his own judgement of the life of Nicholson as the story begins to unfold.

Chapter Two

A Remarkable Heritage

E vidence exists that the historical roots of the Nicholson family can be traced as far back as 1589, the days of the Tudor sovereigns, when three brothers from that family came over to Ireland from Cumberland in the north of England. One was the Rev. William Nicholson M.A., who was married to Lady Elizabeth Percy. He became a Rector in a parish in the County Armagh and County Tyrone areas. Another brother lived in Londonderry and the third in Dublin.

One of the most famous of the Nicholson's descendants was General John Nicholson, hero of Lucknow, whose monument stands in the town square of Lisburn, Co. Down. The Nicholson coat of arms bears the motto "God is my sun." William proudly displayed this motto on his personal note paper.

William Patteson Nicholson was born in Cottown near Bangor on April 3, 1876; he was the fourth son of Captain John G. Nicholson and his wife Ellen. Their family, comprised of four sons and three daughters, was academically bright, and with the encouragement and discipline of their mother they achieved high standards at school.

As a tribute to W.P. Nicholson's family, the Rev. Dr. Henry Montgomery, a lifelong friend of the Nicholson's, wrote:

Mr. Nicholson comes of well-to-do Ulster Presbyterian stock. His grandfather and grandmother were very regular worshippers in the congregation of the late Rev. W. Patteson, of Bangor, a godly and devoted minister of the Gospel, who was often made a blessing to the present writer, and whose memory he cherishes with warm affection. Mr. and Mrs. Campbell (Mr. Nicholson's grandparents) were also warm friends of the minister, and one can recall the regularity with which they attended their place of worship on the Lord's Day, and particularly at the communion seasons. His grandfather (Captain Nicholson) was an earnest Christian man, devoted to prayer meetings and to any good work he could do. Whatever there may be in a worthy ancestry, the Rev. W. P. Nicholson can look back upon his forebears with gratitude to God. He himself was called after the Rev. William Patteson.

The contribution made to Christian work by the other members of the Nicholson family is often overlooked and not fully appreciated. The eldest of the family, Sarah, served as a pioneer missionary in China, the first lady missionary to be sent by the Irish Presbyterian Mission. Dr. J. M. Hunter, a medical doctor serving the Lord in China, had twenty years earlier appealed, "Send some sensible women." Miss Nicholson responded to the call and set sail for that land in 1889 with the hope that other ladies would follow. That hope was not in vain, for by 1906 thirteen others had followed. Their work fell into four areas: teaching, medical work, itinerating and training. The training portion of this work was preparing native women for evangelism. Sarah was appointed to the remote province of Manchuria where she opened a school and held meetings in the town. She eventually married the Rev. Daniel Robertson, a missionary of the United Presbyterian Church of Scotland. Together they travelled throughout the district spreading the good news of the Gospel, and many came to know Christ as Saviour through their evangelistic efforts.

Another of the sons, Dr. James Nicholson, served as a missionary medical doctor for fifteen years with the famous John Gibson Paton

Mission in the south Pacific island of New Hebrides, now Vanuatu. Unfortunately James contracted typhoid fever along with other illnesses and as a result was not permitted to continue his missionary work in the islands. When the First World War broke out, Dr. Nicholson joined the Australian Army, and later in 1916 he and his wife returned home aboard a troopship to Bangor where he began a medical practice.

In 1904, Nellie, a younger daughter, married Mr. James Bowman Hanna, a missionary with the Jungle Tribes Mission. They met while he was on furlough, and she returned with him to India. Conditions there were very difficult, and in 1908 they lost their two children within a two week period. This personal tragedy convinced James of the need for doctors on the mission field; therefore, in 1910 he resigned from the mission and left for Edinburgh University to study medicine. He graduated in 1917 at the age of forty-one and served as an army doctor in Macedonia, Russia and Asia Minor where he attained the rank of Major. Tragically, during this time two more of their children died.

Upon his release from the army in 1920, Dr. Hanna and Nellie were called by the Irish Presbyterian Mission to return to India and for thirty years he served as a medical missionary. He became the medical superintendent of Anand Hospital where he specialised in eye operations. They retired to Bangor in 1950 where they continued in their tradition of hospitality.

Life had not always been smooth; sorrow upon sorrow had plowed furrows that were not visible on the surface, yet they left deep scars on their happiness. But God's faithfulness triumphed so that when trials were past no bitterness remained, and because they had experienced such sorrow and loss they were able to empathize with others and comfort them with their deep understanding.

EARLY CHILDHOOD

William's early childhood was a happy one. He was born near Bangor the seaside town overlooking the North Channel. His father was a sea captain and served in the Merchant Navy. It is little wonder that two of his sons, Louis and William, were filled with a longing for a life at sea. One of William's earliest memories was associated with his first sea voyage from Hull, England to the West Indies which he took when he was only six years old. The return voyage was made to Bremerhaven, Germany where his father spent long days anxiously anticipating the arrival of Mrs. Nicholson from England. It was subsequently learned that the passenger steamer on which she had embarked had lost its propeller in a storm and had drifted helplessly about in the wild North Sea until found by another vessel and towed safely into harbour.

As a young boy he was very proud of his first long voyage and felt greatly superior to his small playmates in his home town, to whom he told again and again of the sights he had seen, and of the adventures he had experienced; doubtless these stories lost nothing in the telling.

ALBERT STREET PRESBYTERIAN CHURCH

Mrs. Nicholson was a very godly influence in the lives of her family. William described how she regularly walked the family a distance of approximately two miles to Albert Street Presbyterian Church twice every Sunday where the Rev. Henry Montgomery exercised a strong evangelistic ministry. He was so direct in his preaching of the Gospel, and his invitations to accept Christ were so forceful that William, under conviction of sin, had to jump over a seat at the end of the services in order to escape the preacher's attempts to win him for Christ.

SCHOOL DAYS

The Nicholsons eventually moved to Fitzroy Avenue, in the Queens University area of Belfast. Turn-of-the-century education was controlled mainly by the churches, and the first school that William attended was in Fisherwick Presbyterian Church. There he was well grounded in the three R's. Complementary to this secular education was religious instruction from the Bible, and from the Shorter Catechism of the Westminister Assembly of Divines. By this means he was schooled in the great doctrines of the Word of God.

After Fisherwick, he continued his education at the Model School in the Falls Road area of the city, and he recalls, "We were taught, clearly and painfully at times, all we needed. They [the teachers] were old fashioned and believed not only in moral persuasion, but in the propulsive power of a new affection, namely a good sally rod—well seasoned. I have warm recollections of this new affection. I am sure I needed it. I would have lost something if I hadn't had it."

About this time he had a bad bout of sea fever and became restless and discontented with school. His ambition was to go to sea and become a sailor; therefore, he played truant from school spending days around the docks looking at the ships and longing to get away in one of them. When his parents found him out and heard of his desire to go to sea they thought a change of pace would dissipate these wild dreams and allowed him leave school and go into business.

Chapter Three

A MODERN DAY PRODIGAL

Having left school William started work as a clerk in the office of Messrs. Edward Shaw and Company, one of Belfast's numerous linen firms. For a time he settled down at home, but the lure of the sea had gripped him, and its call was too strong to resist. At every opportunity he was down by the waters looking with longing eyes at the restless ships, the busy sailors and the far stretches of the sea. He could no longer resist the temptation, and in spite of the efforts of his parents to keep him at home, he found himself at the age of sixteen apprenticed on the large barque Galgorm Castle. He worked on this boat for four years during which time he received no wages, but he earned his new suit with brass buttons and his cap with a gold badge which he wore with pride .

His first experience as a sailor proved a rude awakening from his idyllic dreams of life at sea, for a storm arose at the very beginning of the voyage, and he became seasick and would have given the world to be in his own snug home once more. William himself said that he would have been willing to take any position, however menial, if only he could be on shore again. But it was now too late, and he joined a number of drunken sailors in setting the sails to save the ship from the storm. The rain came down in torrents, and the wind blew madly through the rigging; the ship, in spite of her size, was but a plaything in the raging tumult of wind and water. But God preserved him as He had preserved Jonah and Paul in similar peril. Nicholson soon realised that he was destined to outlive this and many other storms.

UNFORGETTABLE VOYAGE

During his ocean wanderings William had many thrilling adventures. On one particular voyage from England to Valparaiso, South America, coal in the cargo hold shifted while rounding Cape Horn, causing the ship to list heavily to one side. After hours of intense suffering and danger, expecting every moment to be washed into the raging sea or to have the ship turn completely over, the twenty-four men clinging desperately to its side saw a vessel coming toward them at great speed. She soon saw them and hove to, putting off a lifeboat with nine men in it. The lifeboat came as near as it could, but because of the wreckage strewn around them it could not get close enough to actualize the rescue. The crew called on them to jump over-board where they would be plucked out of the water, but the men were stiff and weak, for they had not eaten a bite for twenty-four hours. They were so exhausted that if they had jumped into the high rough seas they would never have reached the boat; they could not even shout. The lifeboat stayed by as long as possible, but when the rescuers realised their efforts were futile, they turned back to their own ship and sailed away.

TERROR OF DEATH

William later reflected on their feeling of hopelessness.

We were all filled with despair. If ever I prayed to God to save me—not from shipwreck, that never entered my head—but to save me from hell, it was then. Oh, it was real. All my boasted infidelity and scorn of religion was gone. I knew that if we were to sink, I would not only be in a watery grave but a burning hell. The fear of hell filled me with terror. I had cursed God and sinned against Him grievously and willfully. When it comes to a time like this, all the doubts and denials and defiance vanish from you, and you know the reality of hell and having to meet God. Laughter and mockery depart like the ass Absalom was riding on when caught by the hair in the branches of a tree.

I noticed that all the other men were feeling as I was. We were like rats caught in a trap. Like cowards we were squealing for mercy. The God we had defied and denied we were now crying to for mercy. I promised Him if He would save me and rescue me from drowning, I would serve Him. As I look back now to that time, I tremble with fear, because as I cried to God, a queer calm came over me, and all fear of hell and judgement passed away. I said to myself, if we are not saved from drowning, my soul is saved from hell.

It was a delusion of the devil. He had filled me with a false peace. If I had been drowned, I would have gone to hell, deluded and damned, because after we were rescued, I continued in sin. I again denied and blasphemed God. I gave myself up to debauchery and wickedness. I laughed at my fears when so near death. Friends, let me warn you who are unsaved. You think you can live in sin and die in peace and go to heaven. If the devil can deceive you now while you are in health of body and mind, do you think he can't deceive you when dying? If he can give you peace now while in health, how much more will he deceive you when you are weak and sick and dying? Be not deceived, "God is not mocked." You can't make a convenience of God, and think you can be saved when you like. Only now is the accepted time. Now is the day of salvation. Tomorrow is but another day. Tomorrow is Eternity.

As a last resort they broke into the hold of the ship and shifted the cargo over to the other side until they got the vessel upright and stable so that the helm could be used. They rigged up some sails on what was left of the masts and turned back round Cape Horn. After some days of drifting, the vessel was picked up by a British man-of-war and towed into Port Stanley, Falkland Islands.

SOWING WILD OATS

After four years Williams apprenticeship expired and he left the merchant navy. He disembarked at the first port which was Cape Town, South Africa. He immediately demanded and was granted his release. He found himself in a large city and a strange land, friendless and broke. William later wrote, "If ever there was a lonely, home-sick man, it was I." While walking up the main street he met another young sailor, and he was surprised and delighted to find he was also from a town near Bangor.

William's new friend got him a job on the railroad as a porter, but he did not like the work, and left to work on the construction of the Cape-to-Cairo railroad. The foreman was glad to get another man; workers were scarce because of the epidemic of blackwater fever. It was common knowledge that every sleeper on the railroad was a white man's grave.

Again William embraced a wild and wicked lifestyle; all restraint was cast away. Most of his work mates were living under assumed names. William admitted, "I was as wild as the rest, but never was free from conviction of sin. I saw so many dying of the fever; twenty-four hours after they were stricken, they died, and I was continually filled with secret dread and terror. In fact, it became unbearable. I felt I would have to be saved if I stayed there any longer. So Satan told me to leave and go south on the railroad, and I could become a Christian. No one would know me. If I became a Christian here (he told me), I would be jeered and sneered at. So off I went—1,800 miles away."

There he chanced to meet a shipmate from a previous voyage and this interruption took his mind off becoming a Christian; how cunning and subtle the old devil is. But after a period his convictions increased, and he could find no rest, peace or satisfaction in the lifestyle he was leading so once again he departed for the north.

While in the north one of his friends became deadly sick. There was not a doctor within a hundred miles. William took it upon himself to do all that he could for the sick man in the miserable heat. He sat at his bedside fanning and caring for him during the night. He was delirious, raving about his mother, boyhood days and home. Toward morning he seemed to be sinking. He wakened, and looking at William said,

'Billy, I can't die; I am not saved, could you help me?' What could I say? I wasn't saved myself and was soaked in liquor at the time. He cried out, 'O God, if you make me well, I will become a Christian and serve Thee.' The amazing thing was that the crisis of the fever passed in his favour, and he got well. This made me more anxious and miserable than ever. A doctor arrived some time after and told him he must clear out, for he couldn't live in that climate. He told me this, and suddenly asked me if I would come home with him. With hardly a thought I said yes. So I gave in my notice and lifted my money, and we started for Cape Town en route home by steamer to Southampton.

When we were nearing the port I began to wonder how I would be received at home. I had caused them much sorrow and shame by my sinful, willful wandering. They hardly knew where I was. They never dreamed I was coming home. I wondered, would they kill the prodigal instead of the calf? I wired I had arrived and was coming home. They couldn't believe it was from me and sent the wire to another family of the same name. When we were crossing over by steamer to Belfast, I wired again; and when I arrived at Belfast, I wired that I was coming by the 11 p.m. train to Bangor. But I made the mistake of putting the time of my arrival as 11 p.m. instead of 11 a.m.

A MOTHER'S WELCOME

When I arrived at Bangor there was no one to meet me. I felt like turning back again. But I thought, while I am here I might as well take a look at the old home. So I made my way there. I passed by the drive way to the house several times, and just as I was making my mind up to go away, my dear old mother came out with a basket of washing to hang on the clothesline to dry. I couldn't help myself; I called, "Mother." She dropped the basket and had me in her arms in no time. My tears and hers blended as she kept saying, "Oh, I am so glad to see you." Over and over again she hugged me and loved me and wept over me—not a word about my sin or sinful life. She was just glad I was home.

Three weeks passed by when one Monday morning I was sitting by the fire reading the morning paper and smoking, while mother was busy preparing the breakfast. Suddenly and without warning a voice said to me, "Now or Never. You must decide for or reject Christ." Sweat broke out on my brow. I trembled all over with fear. In my heart I cried, "Lord, I yield. I repent of all my sin and now accept Thee as my Saviour." Suddenly and powerfully and consciously, I was saved. Such a peace and freedom from fear—such a sweet and sure assurance filled my soul.

I turned to my mother and said, "Mother, I am saved."

She looked at me and nearly collapsed and said, "When?"

I said, "Just now."

"Where?"

"Here, where I am sitting."

She cried with joy unspeakable. She couldn't say a word but just hugged me and cried. Her baby boy had not only come home but was now saved. Happy day, happy day, when Jesus washed my sins away! It was on a Monday at 8.30 a.m., the twenty-second of May 1899. What a day. A day that will never see an end.

William Nicholson was now saved, and he knew it. "I have never had any doubts about my salvation," he declared. "The Blood had been applied and the Spirit answered to the Blood. I never doubted about my dear mother's word about my natural birth, and do you think its strange of me to take God's word without a doubt or fear? I became a new creature and began hating sin."

Later as a great evangelist he often sang the words:

He called me long before I heard,
Before my sinful heart was stirred;
But when I took Him at His Word,
Forgiven He lifted me.

From sinking sand He lifted me;
With tender hand He lifted me;
From shades of night to plains of light;
Oh, praise His Name, He lifted me.

Chapter Four

THE FULLNESS OF THE HOLY SPIRIT

Having accepted Christ as his Saviour, William found himself in the midst of a spiritual crisis. He immediately sent a telegram to his brother James, then a student in Edinburgh University: "Have decided, but am in dense darkness." He felt convinced that full salvation held far more for him than what he was experiencing. He says of himself at this crisis point in his life,

"I blundered on in my half-saved condition for seven months. The peace, joy and assurance continued but in a fluctuating way—sometimes doubting, sometimes trusting, sometimes joyful, sometimes sad. All grosser sins dropped off me, and I had no sorrow about it or any bother with them; but the sins of the flesh and the spirit—envy, jealousy, malice, and hatred, continued to plague me greatly. I could crush them down, but they continued to rise up again more vigorously than ever.

The fear of man was a dreadful snare, and I was helplessly caught by it. I was ashamed of Christ and ashamed of being seen with out-and-out Christians. I was a sneak and a coward if ever there was one. I despised myself but was helpless about it. The fear of what men would say and do if I confessed Christ terrified me.

I attended church twice every Sunday and joined the men's Bible class. I read my Bible but didn't get any good out of it and had little or no desire for it. Prayer was a real penance and seemed useless. What a wretched, miserable experience I was passing through. If I could have given it all up, I believe I would have done so. I wondered, was this all that salvation meant? So many saved ones around seemed to be enjoying the same experience as I. We never heard from the preaching there was any way out. It was, "Do the best you can." "Hitch your wagon to a star." "Each victory will help you," but I rarely, if ever had victory.

I always enjoyed life, even my life of sin. After I was saved, I often fell into sin, but I did not enjoy it. The world renounced had left an aching void, but my salvation didn't seem to fill the void. I am glad in a way that I had to pass through this long seven month experience, because I have helped so many believers who were living the same sort of life out into a life of holiness, happiness and helpfulness. God never intended His people to live wandering in the wilderness. He brought them out of Egypt by blood and power to bring them into Canaan.

UNCONDITIONAL SURRENDER

Thank God, the day of my deliverance was at hand. One of the leading businessmen of the town, an out-and-out man for Christ and souls, arranged for a "Convention for the deepening of the Christian life." He was Mr. S. G. Montgomery, brother of Dr. Henry Montgomery. The Rev. J. Stuart Holden of London was to be the speaker. He and my brother James were close friends in their student days working in connection with the C.C.S.M.

I was invited to attend. I didn't know what sort of a meeting the convention was. I thought it first to be another religious service; so I had no fear about attending. What a surprise I got the very first meeting as I heard Mr. Holden speak. It seemed to me that my brother, or someone, had told him about the failure I was as a Christian. I felt a little annoyed. But I was there the next night, and I felt sure he had been told about me, for he made clear and public my spiritual condition. I was more annoyed than ever and determined I wouldn't attend another meeting.

I was there again the next night, however, when it was made clear to me that Jesus had made full provision for not only my salvation but also for a life of victory over the world, the flesh and the devil. As I had received Jesus Christ as my Saviour by repentance and faith, not of works or merit but on the ground of grace and by faith, so if I would surrender fully laying my all on the altar of sacrifice and receive by faith the Holy Spirit to sanctify and fill me, He would give me a clean heart and possess me fully, and as I continued to walk in the light as He is in the light, that is walk by faith and obedience, the Blood of Jesus Christ His Son would keep on cleansing me from all sin.

It was all so sublimely simple. I was amazed; I thought it could only be attained by hard work, but the gift of the Holy Spirit is an obtainment. I didn't immediately obtain it. I was frightened to make the surrender without any strings attached. It was this unconditional surrender that filled me with fear and hindered me receiving the blessing. The devil was working overtime with me, filling me full of mostly lies. He told me I would have to be a missionary, to leave all and go abroad, or I would have to make a fool of myself in some public way. I would lose my reputation.

Although he was worried about losing his reputation and making a fool of himself publicly, God had already begun to set the stage upon which William would shed his inhibitions.

The Salvation Army had come to our town. The Corps consisted of two wee girls in uniform. They held open-air meetings and made a noise with their tambourines. Their first soldier was a man called Daft Jimmy. He had hardly enough brains to give him a headache, but he had sense enough to get saved. He carried the flag as they marched the streets, and he wore a red knitted jersey with the words "SAVED FROM PUBLIC OPINION" on his back in large white letters. I was told by Satan that I would have to go to the open-air meeting and march down the street with two wee girls and a fool. This filled me with a horrible dread. I would be laughed at by all my friends. I would lose my reputation.

I said, "Lord, I will be willing to go to Timbuktu or Hong Kong or even die decently as a martyr." I couldn't get out of it. I became more and more miserable and oh so hungry for freedom and victory. At last I became desperate. The last night of the convention I realised God would settle for nothing less than a clean cut, unconditional surrender. I must choose between this surrender or a life of wandering in failure, defeat and dissatisfaction. I left the meeting and went down to the shore, and there under a clear sky and shining stars I made the complete, unconditional surrender. I cried out, "Come in. Come in, Holy Spirit. Thy work of great blessing begin. By faith I lay hold of the promise and claim complete victory o'er sin."

Hallelujah! What a thrill; what a peace; what a joy. Although an old-fashioned Presbyterian, I began to weep and sing and rejoice like an old-fashioned Free Methodist. When I came home, I told my mother, "The surrender has been made, and I am free and so happy." She was delighted, for she told me she had wondered whether I was really saved or not. She knew the blessing of the Holy Spirit, for she had received it under the Rev. Andrew Murray's preaching held in a convention in Belfast.

THE VALLEY OF HUMILIATION

The wonder to me was that all the fear of what men might say or do had vanished, and now I was willing to do anything or go anywhere. The very thing I dreaded most before receiving the blessing, walking down the street with the Salvation Army, had to be faced. I couldn't say I was very happy about it, but I told the Lord I would do what He wanted—cost what it may. So I went to their open-air meeting on a Saturday night. This is the night when most of the country people were in town, and just about everybody was out shopping or meeting friends on the street. Any other night of the week the streets were largely deserted. I tried to compromise about the day, but the Lord held me to Saturday.

As I walked down the street that Saturday it seemed as if every friend and relative I ever had were out and about. When I came to the to the open-air meeting and saw the two wee Salvation Army girls singing and rattling their tambourines and poor Daft Jimmy holding the flag, I nearly turned back. Talk about dying. I was dying hard that night; I stepped off the foot path and stood in the ring. The soldiers looked at me. Then to my horror one of them said, "The people don't seem to stop and listen; let us get down on our knees and pray." What could I do? I couldn't run away. So down I got on my knees.

The crowd gathered around. I could hear their laughter and jeers. The officer prayed a telegram prayer—short and to the point. I could have wished the prayer had been as long as the 119th Psalm. I stood up blushing and nervous. They got the collection while the crowd was there, and then to my horror, one of the wee girls said, "Brother, take this tambourine and lead the march down the street to the Barracks." I couldn't let a girl beat me, so I took it. That did it. My shackles fell off, and I was free. My fears were all gone.

I started down the street, whether in the body or out of the body, I can't tell. I lost my reputation and fear of man; joy and peace and glory filled me. I can see now and understand why the Lord dealt with me so drastically. I would never, I believe, have come right through out-and-out for Christ in any other way. I was naturally timid and shy. I lost something that night I never want to find again, and I found something I never want to lose. That is, I lost my reputation and fear of man, and I found the joy and peace of the overflowing fullness of the Spirit. Hallelujah!

> *Oh, the peace my Saviour gives,*
> *Peace I never knew before;*
> *And my way has brighter grown,*
> *Since I learned to trust Him more.*

The next day was the Sabbath, and as a good respectable Presbyterian I got up early, had my breakfast and went forth to Hamilton Road Church where I belonged. I knew I was for it, for the whole town was humming with what happened to me and the way I had danced up the street with the Salvation Army flag. When I came to the door I saw two

elders, and there they stood with their tall hats. I thought that attack
would be the best form of defence, so I walked right up to them and
said. "Hallelujah men!" and they nearly fell down the steps. "What did
you mean by that last night," they asked, "disgracing your religion and
the God of your fathers! Do you think that is adorning the doctrine?" I
laughed, "Ha! ha! ha!" and said, "You just wait your time." Glory to
God, those old men eventually came to sit at my feet in Bangor. I walked
on in and took my seat in my usual pew. The first Psalm was Psalm
twenty-three. And if ever my heart was full, it was full then. I started to
sing, "The Lord's my Shepherd, I'll not want." Of course I was used to
shouting above the gale in the storm at sea, and with the full strength of
my lungs I sang with all my soul, "The Lord's my Shepherd." When I
came to the second verse, I knew something was wrong. And I beheld
in front of me a very respectable lady in a beautiful fur coat, and as I was
singing she turned round, and if looks could have killed me, Wiltons,
the funeral undertakers, would have had a job. I would have been dead.
But my heart was so full I said to myself, "If she does it again I will
teach her a lesson, and she will never turn round in her seat again." So
it came to that verse that says, "My head with oil Thou dost anoint, and
my cup overflows," and she turned round and looked at me again, and I
stuck out my tongue as far as I could. She turned back and never looked
round at me again! I got the victory over respectability, over what men
think or say, over every accusation of the Devil, over every accusation
of the flesh, over every accusation of the world.

In considering William's baptism of the Holy Spirit, several important clarifications must be made. First, he believed the filling of the
Holy Spirit to be a deep and separate experience than that of salvation,
but he did not link this second blessing experience to speaking in tongues.
William preached on this in his sermon *After Pentecost - What?* "The
blessing of a personal Pentecost is always a second subsequent blessing.... In regeneration there is an impartation of life, and the one who
receives it is saved. In the Baptism with the Holy Spirit here is an
impartation of power, and the one who receives it is fitted for service."

Second, he did not limit his experience with the Holy Spirit to a
once-and-for-all experience. Rather he considered it to be a succession

of new empowerings for each new task that the Lord appoints us to do. Like D.L.Moody he considered himself to be a "leaky vessel" and had to live right under the fountain in order to be kept full. In a sermon entitled *Born-Baptised-Filled* he draws the distinction between baptism and the process of being filled. "The baptism with the Holy Spirit is a crisis. The fullness of the Holy Spirit is the process—one baptism, many fillings. There is no end or limit to this fullness. We are being filled increasingly and unceasingly. As our capacity enlarges, our fullness increases. There is no such a thing as a once-and-for-all fullness. We are being fitted and filled unto all the fullness of God, until out of us shall flow rivers—not *a* river, but rivers. Hallelujah! Rivers of love, joy, peace and all the graces of the Spirit."

Third, he did not claim sinless perfection. "Heart purity is not sinless perfection, nor does it put us beyond the possibility of sinning. Old Job said, 'If I should say that I am perfect, I should even prove myself perverse.' (Job 9:20) This blessing of heart-purity puts us where we no longer make any allowance for sin or enter into any secret alliance with sin. We no longer talk about sin being a 'necessary evil.' If it is evil it is not necessary. If it is necessary it is not evil. We abhor all evil and cleave to all good."

William dated his own effectiveness in his Christian service to that night, seven months after his conversion when he surrendered fully, laid all on the altar of sacrifice and was filled with the Holy Spirit.

Chapter Five

FIRST EFFORTS IN SOUL WINNING

U ntil William's baptism of the Holy Spirit, he had been living in defeat. The fear of man had dominated his life, and he had been afraid to witness. But now he was different. He experienced a new power in his life. He now began to enjoy the victorious life.

What a change it wrought in my life. I no longer had difficulty in witnessing for Christ in meetings and to individuals. I began holding meetings in homes—especially working men's kitchens. They would gather around a big peat fire with an oil lamp on one side. There I stood before the fire and the lamp. If I didn't have inspiration, I certainly had perspiration.

One of the first meetings I held, I was sure I had a great sermon; but when I started to speak, all I had prepared vanished and I stood dumb. One dear old lady called out, "Never mind, Mr. Nicholson, you'll do better the next time."

William not only held public meetings but he also witnessed for Christ in the work place.

I got invoicing work in the Railway freight department. I didn't know a thing about invoicing, but I prayed about it. I soon was as fast and accurate as any of them. There were about a dozen of us invoicing, but none were saved. I wondered how I could speak to them about their souls' salvation. The Lord gave me the idea to help them in their work. Some were slow because they were lazy or careless. After I had given them an hour or so of my time, they couldn't very well not listen to my testimony.

I went round each one frequently. They were quite willing to listen to me under the circumstances. I never had the joy of leading one of them to Christ, but the Lord was looking after my best interests as I was busy about His work. I received a note on my desk one morning telling me the head of the department wanted to see me in his private office at 11 a.m. The old devil filled me with fear as I went to his office. He told me there was a good job and more pay in a shipping company's office. He said he had influence there and could get me the job. I wondered why he chose me. Was it to get rid of me? Had I not been doing good work? I thanked him and said, "Sir would you mind telling me why you were interested in me to do this?" I hadn't been a year in the office. Other clerks had been there many years. He said, "I noticed how you went round every department learning their work, so that when any clerk was absent you were able and willing to do their work as well as your own." He said that he was determined to help me get on as I was ambitious and industrious. I told him that my reason for doing as I did, was that I wanted to win them for Christ. He was flabbergasted. I had a good chance for a word with him about his soul, but didn't succeed in winning him for Christ.

William was soon transferred to the accounting department where once again he knew nothing about the work but was eager and willing to learn.

The head of the department was a very bad, cursing, swearing, foul-mouthed sinner. I rebuked him. It made him mad; therefore, I couldn't understand why I received a ten shilling rise weekly, but some time afterwards I discovered why. I had come by train to work as I did every day. One day while reading my Bible in the train a verse got hold of me, "No weapon that is formed against thee shall prosper: and every tongue that shall rise against thee in judgement thou shalt condemn. This is the heritage of the servants of the Lord, and their righteousness is of me, saith the Lord." (Isaiah 54:17) I couldn't tell you how that gripped me. During the day one of the clerks I had led to Christ came to me and said, "Do you know how you got the ten shilling rise some time ago?" I said, "No." He told me that my boss went to the managing director and told him I didn't know anything about accounting. It wasn't fair that such a one should be put in his department. The director asked him only one question, "Is he lazy?" "No," said my boss, "he isn't lazy; I can hardly keep him in work. As long as I explain the work to him, he does it and is asking for more." The director said, "Give him a ten shilling rise and keep him in your department." When I heard this, I rejoiced in my heart and praised God.

When I had the chance, I came to my boss and asked him if he had wondered why I had not been fired but had received a rise of ten shillings? He said he had. I opened my Bible and told him to read Zechariah 2:8 which he did. "For thus saith the Lord of hosts; After the glory hath he sent me unto the nations which spoiled you: for he that toucheth you toucheth the apple of his eye." I explained to him he was touching the apple of God's eye when he was trying to injure me. It put a fear in him, and he was different from then on.

From these experiences I learned the truth of the promise, "Seek ye first (not second or third) the kingdom of God, and His righteousness; and all these things shall be added unto you." (Matthew 6:33) It always pays to serve and love the Lord Jesus. When we put all our affairs into His hands and leave them there, they are safe from all harm and injury. Many times we fall short of realizing this promise because, although we leave everything with Him, we soon undertake our own affairs, and as a result we make an awful mess of things and bring pain, loss and misery to ourselves. "Oh, what peace we often forfeit. Oh, what needless pain we bear, all because we do not carry everything to God in prayer" and leave it there.

WIDENING HORIZONS

I felt a change was coming in my life. I didn't know when or how, but I knew the time would come for me to go out into full-time service. The Rev. J. Stuart Holden and I spent several hours together one day while he was in Ulster. He told me he was sure I would be out in Christian work, but "don't be in a hurry. Wait on God, until you are sure and a door is opened." I didn't tell him I felt the same about my future. I thought it might seem presumptuous on my part.

Waiting time was not wasted time for William. He continued holding meetings, preaching in the open air and distributing gospel tracts. On Sunday afternoons he began evangelistic services in Conlig Orange Hall which is just a few miles outside Bangor. He would visit the homes before hand and invite the people to come to the meeting. He prayed with everyone who would allow him and left them a copy of a Spurgeon sermon. One dear old lady, when asked to attend the service, said, "God love you, Mr. Nicholson, I don't need to go because you speak so loudly the whole village can hear you." His seafaring life had given him a good voice, and when he got warmed up preaching, many said he could be heard more than a mile away.

His dedication in his service for Christ was such that his friends began to recognise the potential of his God given abilities and advised him to prepare more fully for Christian service.

Chapter Six

BIBLE TRAINING

William decided to commence training for the work of preaching the gospel and said goodbye to clerking and applied to the Bible Training Institute in Glasgow. He gave as referees the names of the Rev. W. A. Hill, Mr. John McMeekan and Mr. Samuel Montgomery—all of Bangor. Mr. Montgomery especially had been a great encouragement to him in his Christian life and work, and with the hearty recommendation of these three men he was accepted and entered the Institute on December 19, 1901. He was twenty-six years old.

The Bible Training Institute owed its existence largely to the work and influence of D. L. Moody whose ministry in Scotland bore much fruit. It was established in 1892 by the Glasgow Evangelistic Association; the directors of which invited (at Mr. Moody's suggestion) Mr. John Anderson, a shipping agent of Ardrossan, to assume the duties of principal. Mr. Anderson was the founder of The Ayrshire Christian Union and The Southern Morocco Mission, and from 1892 until 1913 he devoted his unique Bible knowledge and gifts of business ability to the furtherance of the work of the Institute and sought to maintain a spiritual atmosphere among the students. He seemed to sense when the spiritual pulse was low or when their pranks were not altogether becoming. A special session would be called in the Lecture Hall and the flashing eyes and impassioned stricture of the principal brought the students back to a fuller realization of their high and holy calling. Godly John Anderson left his imprint upon many student's lives.

The work of the Bible Training Institute commenced in temporary premises, and by 1898 the imposing premises at 64 Bothwell Street were opened at a cost of over £50,000 provided mainly by the late Lord Overton and his sister. The new building had been three years in use when William Nicholson became a student.

He later described his first impressions of student life. "I have vivid memories of my first few days there. I have always suffered from shyness. Even yet, after fifty years in the ministry, I am afflicted by it every time I enter a pulpit or step onto a platform. After I arrived at the Institute I was shown my wee cubicle containing a single bed, a chair, a table and a dresser. I liked having a private room. The idea of a crowded dormitory was a terror. I was so shy I couldn't face coming to the dining room and meeting all the students, so I fasted and prayed. That day I didn't appear at any meals. I slipped out to a lunch counter instead. A student was sent to my room to see if I was sick. He saw how I felt and took me in charge. As I met my first experience with the staff and students around the dining table, I soon felt at home."

William enjoyed himself at the Institute, but at first he found paying attention to the lectures and taking notes hard work. Especially hard for him were the study periods in his room. His previous seafaring, free and easy lifestyle did not help to prepare him for student habits.

The Bible was the only book used for study. Great men such as Professors Denny, Orr, and Lindsay were brought in to lecture. Ministers, including Dr. Alexander Whyte of Edinburgh, also came. All these men were an inspiration and encouragement to William.

He was greatly surprised and shocked to see how some of the students who had come to the Institute on fire for God and souls soon allowed their fires to die down. This was especially noticeable at the

morning half-hour devotions following united-family-worship led by
the principal. A few verses from the Bible were read; then time was
allotted to open prayer for all who desired to take part. At the beginning
of the session many were eager to engage in prayer, but by and by very
few would pray. The silence and pauses were embarrassing. Some of
the students arranged to ease the situation. This caused William to wonder, but he found out the cause. They were depending on, or substitut-
ing, the lectures they were receiving for private devotions. They were
awakened every morning by an electric bell ringing on every floor. They
were supposed to rise and spend thirty minutes in private devotion before family devotions. No wonder prayer died down. William decided
to help them in this. After the first bell rang, he got hold of a dust pan
and brush and went along the corridors banging the dust pan. The noise
was very disturbing, and many were very annoyed, but he was determined that if they would not rise, they would certainly not be allowed to
sleep. The response to his efforts was varied and loud and not altogether orthodox.

William was always getting into trouble, one way or another. He
recalls how he got into serious trouble with the matron, a fine English
lady, who couldn't quite understand the Scotch or the men from Ulster.
The students had to write down anything they needed for their room and
sign their name and room number. William wrote down his request, and
after signing his name, he wrote Amos 4:11. Later he was called to her
office, and she asked him why he had insulted her. "How?" he asked.
She told him to read the Scripture he had quoted in his letter. It transpired that she had thought he had written verse two, which read, "The
Lord God hath sworn... that He will take you away with hooks, and your
posterity with fish hooks." He nearly burst out laughing but was quick
to point out that he had meant verse eleven which he said was his testimony: "Ye were as a firebrand, plucked out of the burning." She let
him off, but he still felt she had not really forgiven him.

William also recalls his first experience of preaching before the
students in the homiletics class: "One student was selected to preach.
The text was given as you reached the platform. You were given three
minutes to preach. I was selected one session, and the text given me

was Zechariah 1:5, 'Your fathers, where are they?' I said I didn't know who they were, when they were born, or where they were born, or who their parents were, how they lived, or where and when they died. But I was sure of one thing—namely, if they were saved, they were in heaven, but if they were not saved, they were damned and in hell. I sat down in great silence; then they burst out laughing. I was never selected again."

As well as excellent teaching the students received many good opportunities for practical work in the churches and mission halls of Glasgow and the neighbouring towns. The large working-class population and the sin and evil which abounded in this large city gave an opportunity as well as a challenge to men who wanted to make Christ known in all His saving power. Open-air meetings were held in many parts of the city and were particularly numerous on Saturdays and Sundays. Some of the workers used to march singing through the streets, and the Irish men among the students relished this kind of activity. They marched shouting and singing with sandwich boards displaying texts of Scripture front and back. Some played trumpets and concertinas, and others had torches and drums. The Ulster students were particularly interested in the drums, and William relished this job. But one time while carrying his drum, he had the misfortune to put the drumstick through the drumhead; that was his final chance as a drummer.

At certain mission halls, tea was provided on Saturday nights and as the people entered the hall, a teacup and a paper bag with some pastries inside were handed to them. In due course the workers came round with large kettles containing tea with sugar and milk already added. Then proceeded a musical programme followed by a "magic lantern" showing slides which usually depicted some Scriptural theme. The Pilgrim's Progress, the Prodigal Son, the Passover and similar stories formed the substance of the lecture which was followed by an appeal for a decision for Jesus Christ. In this way the message of the Gospel was taught, and many conversions were registered in these gatherings. The Tent Hall in the Saltmarket under superintendent Mr. Robert Logan, and the Bethany Hall in Bridgeton where Mr. Peter McRostie had been in charge since 1901 were foremost in these ministries among the poor and needy of the city. It is of more than a passing interest that this ministry had the support and personal service of a number of leading public figures and businessmen in the Glasgow area. Some such men were Lord Overton, Sir Joseph P. Maclay (subsequently Lord Maclay), Sir John Campbell, and ship builders like Napier and many others. They were not merely figureheads but were actively involved in the work and were often found preaching in the open-air as well as in mission halls and church services.

When the summer holidays came, William returned to Belfast where he became assistant in Albert Street Church, under his former minister the Rev. Henry Montgomery. In this thickly populated industrial district, Henry Montgomery had established an evangelistic and social work among the poor and needy. The Rev. Montgomery had also taken on the work of the Shankhill Road Mission and left his flourishing church to direct this new enterprise. This temporary post gave the new assistant an insight into an evangelistic ministry as well as practical experience in the work, and he was challenged by the extraordinary example of his supervisor. Henry Montgomery had one well known weakness; he was drawn to a crowd like a moth to a flame. He would borrow a box or chair from a nearby house, and up he would get, urging his listeners to repent and believe. After he had broken the ice, he would tell William to get up and speak. When the factory workers were leaving their place of work, it took preaching with simplicity and Holy Ghost power to hold them as they made their way home. Henry told William, "If you can't hold them, you haven't much of a message, and you are not fit to preach."

In this type of work, William began to find his feet. He tells that on Saturday nights the open-air meetings were often held after midnight when the public houses were closing, and the drunks were being evacuated onto the streets. The meetings were often lively and stormy, yet many of the listeners were converted. Counting this work a privilege William recalled, "It was a wonderful summer for me. It gave me a passion to win souls for Christ... but I was tired when I returned to B.T.I."

Returning to Glasgow seemed like a rest after his strenuous summer. The contacts he had made with many people in the work of the

Shankhill Road Mission helped him develop in various ways. "It was good," he wrote, "being back in the Institute and meeting the students once more. I hadn't any difficulty about meeting them again. My shyness didn't prevent me feeling at home among them. It was becoming easier to study, and the many meetings held here and there every week helped to relieve the monotony and kept me from getting dried up."

As the days of preparation came to an end, William was thankful to God for the sound Biblical teaching and practical training he had received while at B.T.I. It was there that he developed a love for the Word of God which became more intense with the passing years. It was said of D.L.Moody that he was "a man of one Book—the Bible," and the Bible-centred institutes that he founded in Chicago and Glasgow have permeated the world with Bible loving preachers, missionaries and Christian workers. Many students went on to accomplish great things for God, and among them was W.P. Nicholson whose impact as an evangelist was to be felt throughout the world.

Chapter Seven

REVIVAL IN LANARKSHIRE

Faced with the question of God's will for his future service William had reached a crossroads in his Christian life. He received numerous invitations which would have immediately led him into full time Christian work, but he did not feel at peace to accept any of them.

Meanwhile William was noticed by the committee of the Lanarkshire Christian Union. They arranged for William to preach at a service at Motherwell on Sunday, February 15, 1903; some members of the committee were present to meet and hear him. They unanimously invited William to become one of the Union's evangelists; he was offered a salary of £70 a year with board, lodgings and travelling expenses. He was asked to commence on June 7 but was unable to enter into full time work until July 5. He immediately began his first mission in the market town of Lanark where a large tent was erected for the full month of meetings.

Despite the usual difficulties of evangelism arising from the people's opposition and indifference to the Gospel, his work in the towns and villages of Lanarkshire proved fruitful. His schedule included tent work in the summer, and during the winter and spring he held services in the churches and halls. The workers in the missions were mostly coal miners and steel workers and were out-and-out in their service for God. They were little concerned with their reputations or what others might think about them as long as they were bringing men and women to a saving knowledge of Christ. In this way they were quite at one with the new evangelist.

At one meeting site a big strong miner came to help with the tent raising. He held the wooden pegs while William hammered them in with a 14 lb. hammer. This type of work is tiring on a cool day, but the warm summer sun added another degree of difficulty. William, wearing dungarees and a singlet, was dressed for the task, and with his sweat soaked work clothes and red face, he did not look much like a preacher. William's helper commented, "The way you are working would put the preacher to shame. I suppose Nicholson will come all dressed up and begin preaching after you have done all the hard work." William never let on who he was but let the man continue talking about the well-fed, fat, lazy preacher who would, in his opinion, "do no good." He told William he wouldn't come near the meetings. After the tent was raised, William said goodbye to the miner and walked away without ever fully disclosing his true identity.

The first meeting was held the next Sunday afternoon, and when William reached the platform, who should he see but the big miner. The man looked up at him in amazement; evidently he could not believe that this well dressed gentleman was the same hard working fellow who just the other day had been soaked with the effort of swinging a 14 lb. hammer. When giving the announcements and introducing himself, William said, "I have something good to tell you about the erecting of the tent." He then related the story of the big miner who had helped him. He spared not a word as he described that afternoon's activities and the cynical comments made about the preacher. He ended his story by disclosing that the miner was there in the tent. William did not name him, but most of the audience knew him to be a notable sinner and had a good laugh, but the big miner did not seem to mind, and by the end of the service he had accepted Christ as his Saviour.

Some years later William wrote, "When we began a mission in a town or village, we weren't there long before we had either a riot or revival. Sometimes we had more riot than revival but never a revival without a riot. I usually had a large bell, and I would march the streets shouting my meetings and the Gospel. The marches through the places were strange. Sandwich boards, back and front, torches with plenty of smoke and smell, cornets, megaphones and drums, were often all going full blast at the same time."

William recalled one place which was a nice, decent religious town. He and his workers caused great annoyance by their unorthodox methods, and they decided to have a parade with the vestments of decency and decorum. They all put on old frock coats and tall silk hats and carried sandwich boards printed with large Scripture texts. William also had a big drum and a large bell, and the group proceeded to march through the town singing Psalms. William recalls, "The crowd following was great and the children noisy. We had no reputation to lose, for we had got rid of that long ago. I nearly collapsed, however, when I saw my sister Sarah coming out of the railway station with her newly-wed husband; they were just arriving from China. They were home on furlough and had come to see me. They nearly collapsed, too; and the poor girl was terribly shocked and ashamed. They turned round and went back to the station.

William recalled,

Isn't it queer how God blessed such tactics and stirred the towns and brought crowds to attend and hear and be saved. God moves in a mysterious way His wonders to perform. He often shocks conventionality and custom and tradition of the elders to accomplish His purposes. He made General Joshua get his army together to conquer Jericho by marching them around the city every day for seven days. They must have seemed like a silly crowd acting ridiculously. Who ever heard of capturing a city this way? It was God's way of doing it, and it succeeded.

God's ways are not our ways. They are as high above our ways as the heavens are above the earth. God took a donkey and made it speak to Balaam, warning him from damning his own soul. Evidently Balaam understood what the donkey was saying. He was angered and refused to do as he was told. He damned his soul by one word; he said, "If I have sinned." If he had left out the "If" and said "I have sinned," he would have been in heaven today instead of being reserved unto the blackness for ever.

In one of our missions I asked the workers to get a good lump of chalk and mark on the pavement from their home to the hall, **Nicholson Mission**, with an arrow pointing the way. They took me literally, for they whitewashed in large letters the name and the arrow. The row was on by the officials for disfiguring the streets. One worker was caught and fined. He came to me and said that he couldn't pay the fine, and would have to go to jail. I encouraged him by saying that he was very fortunate, and should be proud at being jailed. He said, "How's that?" I told him he would be right in the middle of the apostolic succession. We lifted a collection and paid the fine. It was the most economical and successful advertising we did.

Another town would not allow open-air meetings without permission. The places we were allotted were out-of-the-way places where few people passed by. I noticed that men selling things on the streets were not molested as long as they kept moving. I got the workers together with their sandwich boards on them. I marched ahead of the parade ringing the bell and preaching as we marched along but so slowly that you could hardly see us moving. What a crowd gathered along the street. The police couldn't hinder us as long as we kept moving. Our workers testified as they moved along; some gave out tracts; others distributed bills announcing our tent meetings. Many were interested, and many were annoyed at us and shouted very uncomplimentary remarks.

I remember we came to a nice Presbyterian-covenanting town. We had a lovely hall (a memorial to the 1859 revival) which seated several hundred. The first week there I never had more than maybe twenty for an audience, and these were mostly dear old women. The town hardly knew I was there or that I was holding an evangelistic mission. I didn't know what to do. One day I met the town crier ringing his big bell and telling about an auction to be held. It was their way of advertising. I got an inspiration. I gave the crier two shillings and six-pence and asked him to lend me his bell. This happened on a clear, starry, dark night—so nice and quiet everywhere. I didn't tell anyone what I was going to do; they would have been shocked and refused to come with me. I got to the top of the main street, took my coat off and tied the arms around my waist; then I rolled up my sleeves and started down the street ringing the big bell and shouting with all my might, "FIRE! FIRE!" What a commotion! Windows were flung open; doors banged. The people crowded out from their houses to see me tearing down the street roaring like a madman and ringing the bell and shout-ing, "FIRE! FIRE!" They thought the town was on fire. We passed the Wee Free Church. They were holding their weekly prayer meeting with about twelve people; out they came. When I got to the bottom of the street where there was a covenanting memorial, I climbed up on it and cried out with a loud voice, "Hell fire is coming, you covenanting Pres-byterians, and I am trying to keep you out of it." I got some rubbish thrown at me, but I got my crowd and packed my hall. The minister said that any man who would do that to get people under the Gospel—he would stand by him, and he did; he came night after night to the meet-ings. The people said, "If he can go, then we will go too." The minister and I became and remained fast friends until he passed away. He was Rev. Dr. Alexander Smellie who wrote the historical classic *The Men of the Covenant*, a moving story of the Scottish Covenanters.

What prayer meetings we used to have: all-nights and half-nights of prayer. The noise, at times, was entreating and joyful. The way some prayed, you would have thought God was a million miles away or deaf. One night when a big-voiced man was praying, one of the nice, timid, quiet prayer warriors tugged at his coat and said, "Brother, God isn't deaf." "No," said the man, "God isn't deaf, but these sinners seem to be."

One prayed, "Lord, give me a good reputation in hell and with the old devil." This created a laugh. Afterwards, I took him aside and said that he shouldn't say things at prayer to cause us to laugh. He said, "Mr. Nicholson, I didn't say it that way. I had been reading it in the Bible." I asked, "Where?" He turned up Acts 19:13-15, "And the evil spirit answered and said, Jesus I know, and Paul I know; but who are ye?" He said, "I want the devil to know who I am." I couldn't say a word. He was a new convert and had been a great sinner.

While labouring in Strathaven William became known as the "swearing" evangelist. The president of the local Union spoke to him about it, and he replied, "Man o' man, if you only knew how much I have to keep back, you would know how to sympathise with me!"

It was while William was working as an evangelist with the Lanarkshire Christian Union that he met Ellison D. Marshall of Bellshill. Her father was Richard Marshall, J.P., a respected and prosperous business man. Ellison had come to know the Saviour during a time of revival in Bellshill United Presbyterian Church. A local branch of the Christian Endeavour Movement (CEM), commenced by the Rev. R. J. Fleming, provided opportunities for service, and she became active in the work of the CEM, visiting the sick and needy and helping with Gospel work in the district. She met William when he came to Bellshill to conduct a mission, and they were married in 1907.

Sometime after their marriage William was invited by his friend, the Rev. J. Stuart Holden of Portman Square Church, London, to come and hold a mission in the hall connected with his church. He was nervous about going to London, but yielding to Stuart Holden's persuasions, he eventually accepted the invitation. One of the persuasions was the promise of every assistance and support, and he was gratified by the interest and help of a grand group of workers, some of whom were titled. It was a time of blessing, and there was a large number of professed conversions.

In the audience on a number of nights were two strangers, and they came to the vicarage after one of the services. They proved to be Dr. J. Wilbur Chapman and Mr. Charles M. Alexander. They asked if William would like to go to America, to which he assented, providing he was sure it was the directive will of God. They suggested that he should ask the committee of the Union for three months leave of absence; they would be responsible for all expenses. The visit would not involve any preaching, but he would attend meetings and see other evangelists at work in a new continent.

He crossed the Atlantic in a luxury liner which was certainly a marked contrast to his earlier experiences in a sailing vessel. The three months passed quickly, and he was invited to join Dr. Chapman and Mr. Alexander for a series of missions. He agreed to accept the invitation for a three year engagement, and his resignation from the Lanarkshire Christian Union took effect on September 30, 1908.

Thus ended five strenuous but fruitful years in Lanarkshire. There he had seen the grace of God magnified in many lives as souls were miraculously changed, and the work of God revived.

Chapter Eight

THE CHAPMAN AND ALEXANDER MISSIONS

Although William was assured that joining the Chapman-Alexander team was God's will, he soon realised how hard it would be to leave the life he had grown to love with the Lanarkshire Christian Union. In addition, he had a pretty little cottage—comfortably furnished and paid for, and their first-born had just arrived—a little girl. He now began to perceive some of the sacrifices he must face as an evangelist. Possibly the most difficult aspect was leaving his wife and young child. They would have no one to care for them as a husband and a father, and he realised that he would miss out on some of the sweetest years of his daughter's life. But he was greatly comforted by the promise of the Saviour, "There is no man that hath left house, or brethren, or sisters, or father, or mother, or wife, or children, or lands, for my sake, and the gospel's, but he shall receive an hundredfold now in this time, houses, and brethren, and sisters, and mothers, and children, and lands, with persecutions; and in the world to come eternal life." (Mark 10:29-30) Although William took comfort in this promise, he was not able to overlook the fact that the promises included persecutions.

Because the Chapman-Alexander Mission was due to commence with a campaign in Melbourne in May, it was necessary for William to leave in March. He embarked from London on the *S.S. Ophir*. Although the vessel was crowded, he did not know a single person on board. Many were waving good-bye to their friends, but there was no one at the dock to wish him good-bye. He describes his feelings, "I had a real dose of mental malaria, ingrowing thoughts and blues. In fact it was a good dose of the old fashioned 'dumps'. The devil succeeded for a while in making me a purebred unbelieving believer."

After getting over this initial attack of the blues, he enjoyed the trip. He spent most of his days on the upper deck in a deck chair with his Bible and books, but because of an early epidemic of sea-sickness, which he escaped, he had very little company. As he sat there alone he pondered what spiritual work could be done among the passengers he would meet. He prayed that when the time came he would have wisdom, courage and tact as he sought to witness. As the Bay of Biscay slid into the distance the heat from the sun replaced the cold of the northern seas and the decks soon became crowded again. Games were soon in full swing, and passengers got to know each other quickly. Aboard a passenger liner people get to know each other's names, where they come from, their business and where they are going. Acquiring this type of information under ordinary conditions would take years, but on a ship many barriers are broken down.

William's prayers were soon answered, and he often found himself talking with his fellow travellers about eternal things. Some had a personal knowledge of the Saviour and enjoyed these discussions, but many found such conversations irksome and avoided further contact as much as possible. He met one young man from the Royal Navy who was out-and-out for God, and they became close friends. They found a quiet place on the deck near the lifeboats where they could talk and pray together and fellowship in the things of God. They were not allowed to hold a service on the first or second class decks, and any request to hold one on the third class deck was likely to be refused, but they decided to hold services in third class without asking and did so on many occasions. The third class passengers were glad to sit around them and sing hymns, and many of those from both first and second class stood along the rail of their decks and listened to the others as they sang and preached. Perhaps this third class method resulted in their ministry reaching more passengers than would have been possible had the services been held on the first or second class decks.

William recalled meeting one young man who was going out to become an assistant minister in a big city church. He had no knowledge of personal salvation and considered that he would have to merit it instead of receiving it by faith on the ground of God's free grace. He was typical of many on that ship—decent, respectable and religious, but without Christ.

Naples proved to be a memorable place of testing and proving for both William and his young friend from the Royal Navy. Early one Sunday morning large parties were arranged for a visit to the ruins of Pompeii. William described the scene, "It seemed as if my navy friend and I were the only ones left on board. When they asked us if we were going, we said, "No." They asked us why. We said it was the Lord's day, and we could not go joy riding on that day. They looked at us as if we were crazy. Some felt guilty and were annoyed at our attitude and testimony. But what else could we do? We had been preaching on board. We could not preach one thing and practice another. We would have ruined our testimony if we had yielded to the old devil's temptation, and our preaching would have been in vain. The Lord made it up to us by filling our hearts with His peace and joy and making Himself very precious and real."

The voyage was soon underway again and before long the steamer arrived at Freemantle, West Australia. Although William would have preferred to continue the journey by boat, he had to leave the boat and take the train to Melbourne to be in time for the beginning of the campaign there. The Chapman-Alexander team arrived in Australia on April 17, 1909; they were later joined by Dr. Ford O. Ottman assisted by Frank Dickson as song leader and soloist and Mr. J. Raymond Hemminger, the Gospel singer who took charge of the music for William.

The spiritual life of Australia was at high tide just at that time. The results of the previous Torrey-Alexander Mission seven years earlier were very evident, and a fresh quickening had been brought by the short visit of Charles Alexander in 1907. There was a great sense of expectancy as the evangelists arrived. With the thousands of prayers going up from the United States and Canada, as well as from all parts of Australia, it was to be a time of Pentecost for the whole Commonwealth.

On arriving in Melbourne, William felt both lonely and homesick and wondered how he would get on. The other members of the team were all men of long experience and great ability, and their names were well-known. William felt that the best thing to do would be to keep silent among them and to watch their mannerisms and their methods of evangelism. He recalls how his sufficiency was in God. He was not dependent on himself in any way. His constant cry to the Lord was:

Oh, to be nothing, nothing;
Only to lie at His feet.
A broken and empty vessel,
For the Master's use made meet.

The evangelistic committee had divided the city into districts, and all the churches in each district united together in a large central hall for the meetings of the campaign. William, along with his song leader, was appointed to Collingswood, a large industrial area. Their meetings were held in the town hall, a beautiful building which seated about 2,000, with large rooms available for dealing with enquirers.

Just before the mission began, Mr. Alexander, who took a personal interest in William, spoke to him about his appearance. He thought that he looked and dressed too much like a country boy and decided to have him fitted for a frock coat and striped trousers as well as a silk hat. At first William felt uncomfortable it his new attire and recalled, "I hardly knew myself. It nearly spoiled me, for I wondered if I would have to preach according to the dress. The Lord delivered and enabled me to forget all about how I was dressed and to seek only to please Him and lead saved ones into yielded, Spirit-filled lives and sinners to the Saviour."

CROWDED MEETINGS

Every night they filled not only the town hall but also the Episcopal church and the Methodist church. Every evening they began in the Episcopal church. His song-leader commenced the service, and while

William preached, he went on to start the service in the Methodist church until William arrived there; they finally finished at the town hall. William rarely preached less than an hour, indeed most times longer. He commented, "When you are in the midst of a revival, the clock is not considered. The Lord beats the devil every way. He can satisfy every longing. His pleasures wear well and satisfy fully."

In spite of the crowded meetings, the secular press gave little or no notice of any of the meetings anywhere. At a noon-day meeting which was held for men-only every day in the Melbourne City town hall, Dr. Chapman remarked that it was strange that the daily papers were taking no notice of the meetings when thousands of the people were interested in them. He suggested that it would work wonders if the business men would phone their papers or write to the editors telling them that if they would not take notice of the meetings, they would cancel their subscription. The men wrote their letters, and reporters were in every meeting of the city that very night and throughout the remainder of the mission.

When William arrived at the town hall that night, he saw a table directly under the platform upon which several reporters were at work. It unnerved him for a time, but he soon forgot all about them. The hall was crowded with people sitting and standing everywhere. They had been there for over two hours. William said that "the atmosphere was like pea soup, but didn't smell like soup. If I hadn't any inspiration, I had plenty of perspiration." He preached that night on the subject "God's Hell". The Holy Spirit began working. He had not been preaching long when some fainted and had to be carried out, causing great confusion in the crowd. But this confusion did not hinder the Holy Spirit convicting or William preaching, and many souls were converted that night.

The next day the leading morning papers had large headlines about the service, such as: APPALLING SCENES; LURID EVANGELIST; THE HORRORS OF HELL PREACHED, etc. It created no small stir. Everywhere William went holding meetings, he was referred to as the hell-fire preacher. One would have thought that hell-fire was the only subject he preached on. Some of the party thought it was an unenviable notoriety. William was not pleased with their reaction. The Lord Jesus made Himself of no reputation, and as long as he had the Lord's approval, he was not concerned about the opinions of others.

FAREWELL MEETINGS

After visiting most of the large cities in Australia, Chapman and Alexander left for the Orient en route to America where they were to begin a mission in Chicago, but William and the others remained behind until the month of August. The day before their departure, they held an entire day of farewell meetings in Brisbane. There was a meeting for ministers at 10 a.m., a businessmen's meeting at 12 noon, a Bible reading at 3 p.m., and the final farewell meeting in the Methodist Church at 7 p.m.

After the long day of meetings, they were thankful to get some time to relax for a few days at Bundaberg where some friends, the Youngs, had a large sugar plantation and sugar refinery. One day while out horseback riding, a kangaroo jumped out of the bush, and the party started to chase after it. William's horse was off before he had got a good hold of the reins, and as it galloped under the branches of a large tree, he put out his hand to protect his face, but unfortunately his wrist was broken. He thought it was just a sprain and did not mention it to anyone. They had to leave on the night train for Brisbane, and the engineer, who had recently been converted, chatted to William before they left the station. He saw the swollen hand and invited him to ride in the engine car; the engineer made William keep his hand in a bucket of cold water in an effort to reduce the swelling. The next morning they were in time for breakfast and a minister's meeting. One of the ministers noticed William's swollen hand and advised him to see a specialist who put a large wooden splint over his hand and along his arm. He could not get his arm into his coat sleeve, so he kept it hidden under his coat while he was preaching. At the evening service, he got warmed up during the preaching and without thinking, out went his arm in bandage and splint into the air. There was a shocked surprise and a burst of laughter from the audience. After the meeting, the doctor took him to his private hospital for the night and eased the pain and the swelling with hot packs. The next morning he took him to the steamer and put him into the care of the ship's doctor.

The group soon set sail for Vancouver, British Columbia. They had a pleasant passage over the Pacific and were able to call at Fiji, Samoa and Honolulu. William had previously sailed through the Pacific in a sailing ship, but what a difference the luxury liner made! At Honolulu the doctor removed the splint and found the broken wrist well healed but a little stiff. On arrival at Vancouver they boarded a train and travelled through Canada, arriving in Chicago in good time to join Chapman and Alexander for the great city-wide campaign. There were seventy evangelists, and as in Australia, each was allotted a certain district where all the churches united in a hall or church. Chicago was then a scattered city of two million people, and to give unity to the campaign, the workers met daily at noon in the Opera House. William's district was called "Little Hell," and it was said that it was not safe to go there without police protection, especially at night. But thankfully they were never attacked or harmed in any way, and indeed they had the great joy of seeing many converted.

Although the campaign was well organized and a tremendous effort had been made, the Chicago campaign never really made any noticeable impact on the city as a whole. There had been disunity among the workers who had been called in from all over America and Great Britain. They were not all with one accord in the one place. William felt that the Holy Spirit's presence and power were not manifested. He commented, "the Lord does not demand unanimity, but does demand unity."

The party left Chicago for Indiana, and while there William received a cable from Pastor D. J. Findlay of Glasgow, asking him to take over the pastorate of the Tabernacle. He had suffered a breakdown in health, and the church was sending him and his wife on a world tour, to visit the mission stations and missionaries connected with the Tabernacle. William was delighted with the invitation as it would mean he would be home with his wife and child as well as having the honour and privilege of carrying on the work while the pastor was away. He was fearful for a time that it was his pleasure he was considering more than the will of God, but after waiting patiently for some time, he received the assurance and peace that he was praying for, and he cabled his acceptance.

Chapter Nine

MILESTONES

The year in Glasgow was a memorable one. The congregation was full of wonderful people who took William to their hearts and gave him help and encouragement. He issued a "pastoral letter," asking the people for their earnest prayers on his behalf for the work of the Tabernacle. There was a perforated part of the letter on which they could fill in their name and address and send it to him. The response was astonishing and heart cheering.

The Tabernacle, which seated about 1,200, was well filled every Sunday, both morning and evening, summer and winter. Every service was preceded by a prayer meeting, and these meetings were never dry nor stiff. The prayers were fervent, short and loud. Many half nights and all nights of prayer were held, and after these prolonged periods of prayer, the fire from heaven truly fell. The results of these prayer meetings were seen in the Sunday services. Almost 1,000 people passed through the enquiry rooms that year. There were also many open-air meetings and marches, and many souls were won for the Saviour. If ever a pastor was upheld and loved by the people, it was William. He never asked them to do anything, but they were always willing. It was a year never to be forgotten, but it had to come to an end.

Pastor Findlay returned to take up the work again, and William made arrangements to return to America. In a way, he was glad to get away from the settled work of the pastorate and take up the work of an evangelist again. He said, "I do not believe that it is ever God's will to put a square man into a round hole, or vice versa. He made me for an itinerant sort of life. So I feel very much at home and enjoy the journeying here and there doing God's work. To be a whole year in one place is a queer strain on my nature and the grace of God in me." The pastor and people invited him to stay with them, but he had itchy feet as well as the assurance that God's will compelled him to return to America. There was a great welcome home meeting in the Tabernacle for Pastor and Mrs. Findlay which was also a farewell service for evangelist W. P. Nicholson who had held the fort so faithfully during the pastor's long absence.

In the month of January, William was back in the U.S.A. holding tabernacle meetings. The churches of a city would unite together and build a wooden tabernacle for the gatherings. These wooden tabernacles were neutral ground, and all the churches felt free to go there. William was assisted by Mr. Raymond Hemmings, the song leader and soloist who had been with him in Australia; several other workers also joined them. The Lord graciously blessed their efforts, and they were kept busy.

VISIT TO MOODY MEMORIAL CHURCH

D. L. Moody died on December 22, 1899, the same year in which William was converted. When William was invited by the Moody Memorial Church in Chicago to hold a gospel campaign there, he considered it a great honour. He was treated with great respect, and while there he was offered the bedroom of D. L. Moody.

The Lord gave a rich time of blessing to both saint and sinner. The church seated 2,200 people—twelve hundred on the main floor and one thousand on the gallery. The church sought to reach all classes, as the sign above the door indicated, "Ever welcome to this house of God are strangers and the poor." The meetings were crowded out, and over-flow meetings were held in the lower auditorium; many souls came to trust Christ as their Saviour, and others dedicated their lives to the Lord.

The song leader for the mission was the director of the music department of the Bible Institute, Dr. D. B. Towner, who has been rec-ognized as one of the world's most prolific gospel song writers. Among his published compositions, which number more than two thousand, are *Anywhere with Jesus, Trust and Obey, Only a Sinner, Redeemed* and *Grace that is Greater than Our Sins.*

One man who became a very dear friend to William was Mr. Thomas Smith. They looked very much alike, and sometimes after a meeting, some of the congregation would come up to Mr. Smith and say, "Mr. Nicholson we enjoyed your message today." William did not know whether Thomas felt it was a compliment or not. Thomas had large apple orchards, and on different occasions they would walk among the trees, and he would tell William about them and share with him some of the lessons which could be applied to spiritual growth and progress. For instance, he once took his knife and cut open the bark of a tree. William wondered why, and he explained that the tree was bark-bound, which meant the sap could not freely flow, and this hindered fruit bearing. This reminded him of the Saviour's words in John 15:2, "...and every branch that beareth fruit, He purgeth it, that it may bring forth more fruit."

Some days later when they were walking in an orchard full of Northern Spy apple trees, they came across several rows of trees that were unlike the others. William asked him why the branches of these trees were all growing up straight, whereas most of the other trees had their branches bent down. He said that the trees whose branches were straight up were young trees and had not yet borne any fruit. When trees bear fruit the branches bend down. William likened this to the Christian who, when he bears fruit, is bowed down and humble. William's cry to the Lord was that he would be a fruitful branch of the vine.

ORDINATION TO THE MINISTRY

During the forty-five years between the founding of the A. B. Simpson's Institute in 1889 and the establishment of Bob Jones College in 1927 there was a phenomenal growth of Bible institutes and colleges; some fifty-five were founded. D. L. Moody had called for the training of "gap-men"—men to stand between the laity and the ministers. Many of these gap-men became very successful evangelists. Others however, refused to join any church, and they created difficulties by their actions and lack of credibility. It was because of this situation that William decided to apply to the Carlisle Presbytery of the United Presbyterian Church for ordination.

According to the April 14, 1914 minutes of the Presbytery of Carlisle, Mr. William P. Nicholson, "an evangelist, a member of the First Church of Carlisle, a student of theology, was invited to present himself with view to examination for licensure and ordination." The next day, by unanimous vote, the Presbytery received Mr. Nicholson under care after due examination. "By unanimous vote the rules with reference to licensure, so far as exceptions have to be taken in the case of Mr. W. P. Nicholson, evangelist, were suspended. Mr. Nicholson preached a trial sermon from Acts 16:31 and was examined in theology and the sacraments. On roll call the examination was, as a whole, sustained, and Mr. Nicholson was ordained as an evangelist in a prayer led by the Moderator and with the laying on of the hands of the Presbytery. A charge to the evangelist was delivered by the Rev. J. G. Rose D.D., and on motion Mr. Nicholson's name was placed on the roll." Dr. Henry Montgomery also took part in the ordination act.

William's comment on his ordination was, "I don't know that it added anything to me or the work. But it did give me a standing. They knew now I was no 'wild-cat' irresponsible sort of evangelist. I came across some evangelists who, when asked what church they belonged to, would say, 'I belong to the Lord.' I always felt a wee bit suspicious about them. I remember in one place where they wanted me for a meeting; the minister said he would have to get the permission of the Bishop. When he consulted the Bishop, he said, 'If he is an ordained man, it will be all right.' I sent him my letter of credence which satisfied him. He had only one condition: I was not to ask the congregation to whistle! So we held the meeting without whistling, but we had plenty of singing and shouting and laughter. Hallelujah!"

William frequently said, "I have had a three-fold ordination— ordained to eternal life, ordained to bring forth fruit, and ordained by Presbytery."

BIOLA

Four years later, towards the end of World War I in 1918, when William was forty-two years old, he was invited to join the staff of the Los Angeles Bible Institute (nicknamed Biola), a large interdenominational college for the training of Christian workers and missionaries. He accepted the invitation and began working with the Extension Department which involved considerable travelling, evangelistic work and Bible conference ministry as well as the presentation of the needs of the Institute to the churches.

That year the student body of the Institute totaled 506, and was represented by thirty-eight States, twenty-seven foreign countries and fifty-eight denominations. The Dean of the institute was Dr. R. A. Torrey, the famous evangelist and author. Dr. Torrey was pleased to commend William as an extension evangelist of the Institute and wrote, "I have followed the work of William P. Nicholson for several years with great interest. I have heard him preach, and he has held a campaign in the Moody church in Chicago, of which I was formerly pastor. I have made many inquiries about him and his work there, and I find that everyone has nothing but good to say about him and his work. Mr. Nicholson is sound in his doctrine, careful in his methods, thorough in his work and leaves a good impression upon a city after he has visited it."

The years spent working as an evangelist for the Institute were but part of God's plan in preparing His servant for a series of missions that was to make his name a household word in the North of Ireland and to help turn the six counties of Ulster from civil war to revival victory.

Chapter Ten

THREE GLORIOUS YEARS OF REVIVAL

W. P. Nicholson was born seventeen years after the 1859 revival, and the fruits of this revival were still being enjoyed in Ulster. The awakening begun by the revival was kept alive by the visit of the American evangelist D. L. Moody to Ulster in the autumn of 1874. Moody himself was a convert of the 1858 revival in America.

Moody's mission had a profound influence upon the spiritual life of God's church and on its outreach in evangelism. His missions also led to the popularity of gospel hymns and to the acceptance and use of the organ. Moody also introduced the practise of the enquiry room. His influence continued in the lives of the next generation of ministers; for example, Dr. Henry Montgomery testified that it was under D. L. Moody's ministry that he "got loosed."

The missions of Dr. R. A. Torrey and Alexander in 1903 also helped to keep alive the blessing of the "year of grace." In accordance with the Torrey mission, the General Assembly of the Presbyterian Church called the church to prayer and exhorted its ministers and members "to give themselves to earnest prayer for a wide spread revival of religion."

During the years of 1904-1905 the land of Wales experienced a great spiritual revival when God answered the prayers of a young coal miner, Evan Roberts, who prayed that God would "bend the church and save the world." Sparks from the heavenly fire of the Welsh Revival began to kindle flames of revival in parts of Ulster. These spots of revival became known as "particular revivals" in Lurgan, Cullybackey, Tobermore and Ballymena.

The Golden Jubilee celebration of the 1859 Revival took place in 1909 and contributed much to the atmosphere of revival in Ulster with many ministers preaching on the subject. As an outcome of these meetings, the General Assembly recorded their thanks to God for the many tokens of His grace bestowed upon the church "which remind us in some measure of the marvellous year of grace in 1859."

The outbreak of World War I in August 1914 changed the everyday life of everyone in Northern Ireland. Thousands of young men from all over the country went forth to fight the nation's battle; many of them were never to return. The loss of a whole division in the Battle of the Somme on July 1, 1916, brought deep sorrow to nearly every home in the land. Everyone prayed for an end to the war, but when the end did come other problems began to surface.

The years after the war saw the province dispirited because of unemployment and mass emigration. The Home Rule issue from the south of Ireland which had faced the people regularly since the 1880's had been checked for a time under Edward Carson's leadership in 1912. But the republican uprising in Dublin at Easter 1916 had embarrassed the British Government and led to a promise from Prime Minister Lloyd George of statehood for Ireland at the end of the war in return for a truce. Lloyd George's solution of the problem by means of the partition has been referred to as the blunder of a sick man and was a solution that nobody wanted. The establishment of a separate Parliament for Northern Ireland comprised of the six north-eastern counties and the granting of Dominion status for the other twenty-six counties under the title of the Irish Free State, now called the Irish Republic, left the country in a state of political turmoil and uncertainty.

The province of Ulster was filled with a sense of fear and of hopelessness. It was at this time that William returned to Ulster from Scotland where he had been invited to conduct a series of missions in commemoration of two sons of Sir Joseph Maclay; both sons had been killed in the Great War. These missions were held during the winter of 1920-21 under the organization of the Glasgow United Evangelistic Association.

Upon his arrival William returned to his home in Bangor to visit his elderly mother and to recuperate from an appendix operation. His old friend and Bible class teacher, Mr. S. G. Montgomery, persuaded him to hold a mission in his home town. This he did in October 1920, in Hamilton Road Presbyterian Church, and hundreds of men and women were converted to Christ. This mission heralded the beginning of a new revival and spiritual awakening throughout Ulster. The Bangor Christian Workers Society's Annual Report stated, "It will ever stand out as an epoch in the history of Bangor, as a time of the most outstanding revival and awakening in the last century." Invitations came from other churches across the province, but William was unable to accept these invitations because of his previous commitment to Scotland.

Towards the end of January 1921 he interrupted his six month campaign in Glasgow, to pay a return visit to Bangor for a short series of meetings. The local newspaper, *The Spectator*, reported, "All meetings noted for unprecedented attendance."

It might be helpful for historical reasons to list here in chronological order the series of meetings of the United Missions, along with their results, which William conducted in Ulster following the first meeting in his home town of Bangor.

Portadown: In May 1921 William commenced a united mission in Portadown; this mission had wide support from all the local churches. The meetings were held in the First Presbyterian Church for the first two weeks then in Thomas Street Methodist Church for the final two weeks. The commencement of the mission was delayed for a week because of the great coal strike combined with a dock strike which delayed William's crossing from Glasgow. The *Belfast Telegraph* interviewed William when he was eighty-two years old, and William laughed as he recalled the beginning of the mission. "We were very fortunate, for there was a shortage of coal and the people of Portadown were kept warm in my mission hall."

The church was packed to capacity for the first two weeks, and this was repeated in the second half of the mission held in Thomas Street Methodist Church. A report of the mission which appeared in *The Irish Endeavour* in July 1921, states:

Mr. Nicholson gained the ear of the people in a marked degree, and although uncompromising in his condemnation of smoking and dancing and the picture show, and presenting the bald alternatives of "Christ or Hell," even those who disagreed with him came under his spell and were converted. Over 900 names were registered as of those accepting Christ and whole families became one in Him.

Another report in the same paper tells of many of the new converts being "notable brands plucked from the burning, and they make no secret of their changed lives."

Lurgan: The following September a mission was held in High Street Presbyterian Church, and nearly 1,000 people came to know the Lord. One report speaks of the town having had a "tremendous upheaval" through the mission.

Under the leadership of Pastor F. H. Forbes, many Baptists shared in the blessing of the mission. Early in the mission William called upon Christians to surrender themselves wholly to the Lord. Mr. Forbes was present on that occasion and went forward publicly to rededicate his life to God's service. He told with some amusement of a report being spread around the town that, "the Baptist pastor had been converted at Mr. Nicholson's meeting."

The experience of revival left a permanent mark on Mr. Forbes. He forever possessed that inner spiritual life of prayer and never lost the burden for the salvation of sinners—the hallmark of those privileged to share in an outpouring of the Holy Spirit.

Newtownards: In November a mission followed in Strean Presbyterian Church, but the attendance was so great, the meetings were moved to the larger First Presbyterian Church. One elderly man who remembered the 1859 revival, said that some of the effects of the Holy Spirit's working even exceeded what happened in '59.

A report by one of the workers reads:

A band of seventy voluntary workers from the various churches were employed as ushers, enquiry room attendants, booksellers and pew watchers. It was the duty of the latter to get in touch with any person who appeared to be anxious and seek to lead them out. I would say in this respect I had the great joy of seeing two to whom I spoke turn back and wait for the after-meeting, at which they came out for the Lord. One of these is a very bright young Christian and a really active worker. For about three weeks there was an average of fifty each night passing through the enquiry room, some truly remarkable cases being amongst these. That the Lord is no respecter of persons was clearly seen by the varied types of sinners who sought Eternal Life. On the last Sunday exactly 117 signed the decision card. The latter is similar to that used in 1859. After the mission 350 decision card tear-offs were sent to the Presbyterian Church, and 250, 140 and 100 to three other churches in the town.

It is said that when William was conducting the mission in Newtownards he went into a certain shop to make a purchase and in conversation asked the shopkeeper if he had been to any of the meetings. The shopkeeper said that he wasn't impressed with that sort of religion. It was all very well for some people to hurry off to meetings, sing hymns and make a great fuss of their devotion, but he knew how many of them owed him money which he never expected to collect. William was concerned and asked if he might borrow the shopkeepers ledger.

That evening at the mission meeting he held the book aloft and explained that it was the accounts receivable ledger of a shop in town.

He didn't say which shop it was, but he did say some things about honesty and the payment of debts, and added that he would borrow the book again the following week at which time he would read the names of the debtors and the amounts they owed.

Everybody was perfectly sure that he was capable of doing just that. Never was there such a rush in the town to settle debts! The shopkeeper who loaned William the book and a number of other shopkeepers as well were most impressed with Mr. Nicholson's brand of religion.

Lisburn: After a short break another mission followed in the Orange Hall and Railway Street Presbyterian Church. An account entitled *Revival in Lisburn* by the Rev. J. N. Spence of the Methodist Church appeared in the Irish Christian Advocate:

Not within the memory of the oldest inhabitant has Lisburn been so deeply stirred as during the United Mission conducted by the Rev. W. P. Nicholson of Los Angeles. For the first ten days, Mr. Nicholson's sermons were addressed to Christians, emphasizing the necessity for the baptism of the Holy Spirit as a separable and separate blessing. With true Methodist emphasis, the doctrine was enforced, and many hundreds claimed the promise of the life abundant. Night after night it was a thrilling sight to see scores of men and women, old and young spring to their feet in response to the missioner's appeal for instant decision for Christ and with up-lifted hand shout, "I will." Mr. Nicholson is blessedly unconventional in his methods, saying daring things, using blunt words but all combining to give a vividness and fire to the message which rams it home to conscience and heart. It is still far too early to speak of the ultimate results of the mission.

Over 2,000 souls definitely pledged themselves to Jesus Christ; 1,950 were dealt with in the enquiry room; over 700 names were transferred to the minister of one church in Lisburn. There was suddenly more members than seating capacity of the building. All other churches have had large numbers of their members converted. In the congregations of our own circuit almost 100 persons have professed conversion.... The whole movement was aptly described by one of our godly members when she said, "It was a miracle that was happening in Lisburn.:"

Belfast: The Shankhill Road mission was held when the political troubles and bloodshed were at their worst in the city; people travelling by tram to the mission had to lie on the floorboards to avoid being hit by rifle bullets. Gunfire could be heard during the services. The invitation to Nicholson was extended by Dr. Henry Montgomery who had carried on an evangelistic and social work for a quarter of a century in the area. The first meeting was held in the Albert Hall on the Sunday evening of February 11. Before Mr. Nicholson preached in the Albert Hall, he conducted meetings in two other neighbouring churches—Townsend Street Presbyterian in the morning and Agnes Street Methodist Church in the afternoon. A report in the *Belfast Newsletter* states that the hall was crowed with a most attentive audience, and the sermon was a rousing appeal to church members. Every available corner was occupied and those who could not find a seat stood throughout the entire service. As for the forty-five minute sermon, "there was not a dull moment during its entire delivery, and many were profoundly moved." A subsequent report in the *Belfast Newsletter* speaks of the services being, "quite phenomenal in their character." Another report in the same paper speaks of the sermon producing, "a deep impression on the congregation and that the after-meeting was crowded."

There were still many people who mocked Mr. Nicholson and were angry at the work he was doing. One man who had heard much criticism of William said, "I do not think it is fair to condemn a man until one has heard him for oneself." When he visited a subsequent service he was one of the first to rise to the appeal and say, "I will." One commentator said of the mission that he had never seen so widespread interest in the area since the days of D. L. Moody. The report of the Shankhill Road Mission Committee to the General Assembly of 1922 states: "The Rev. W. P. Nicholson conducted a very successful mission in the Albert Hall which was packed every evening with close to 3000 people; 2260 men, women and young people passed through the enquiry rooms, and nearly all these were led, it is believed, to a definite decision for Christ."

After a weeks rest William moved to Newington Presbyterian Church in the Limestone Road area of Belfast. A history of Newington Presbyterian Church was written by Dr. Johnstone in 1926; in this account he recorded his impressions of the evangelist and the mission:

This mission was held in March, 1922. On some evenings there were 2,000 people jammed within the church. Aisles, porches, vestibules and windows were crammed. At the first Session meeting, held afterwards, it is recorded that, "As far as it was possible to tabulate, the converts of the Mission numbered 1,100." I was present at every meeting of the series, except one, and though it must be confessed that he studiously spoke more bluntly than any man I have ever heard, yet I cannot recall him ever saying a single one of the other things with which rumour has associated him. The strange things he spoke, he did purposely to gather the crowd. But when he got down to the actual work of preaching, one quickly realised that he had no necessity to adopt any adventitious aids. He was an arousing and convincing speaker. Possessed of a rich voice, an attractive personality, and a very effective form of appeal, he got home to many a heart that, only for him, might have long wandered in the ways of evil. And though as in all mission enquiry rooms, thousands have a way of thinning down into hundreds, and hundreds into tens; nevertheless a work was done in Newington on this occasion of greater or less proportions that will stand the test of time. Apple trees shed many of their blossoms, and only a fragment of spring's early promises ripen to harvest. Yet one has never heard of farmers going out of the business because it is so. They continue for the sake of the few that fulfill their promise. And that is a parable. Again and again Newington congregation has had proofs of how God blesses these special agencies. And if there were no others, surely we have here an instance of effective evangelism.

Londonderry: After the mission in Newington and a short rest, William travelled to Londonderry, where his next campaign was to be held. Again he had a wide measure of support from the churches for the six weeks of meetings which began first in the Methodist Clooney Hall on the Waterside for three weeks and continued in the First Presbyterian Church within the city wall on the west side of the River Foyle.

An account in the Methodist weekly, the *Irish Christian Advocate* reports:

We have had an appalling year in some respects, but spiritually it has been glorious. The winds of God have been blowing over us, and not for many years has our church had so fruitful a season. There are manifest signs of a new spirit in our church. We believe that the revival of spiritual religion in which we are finding ourselves has had much to do with the increased interest in world evangelism.

Professor James Strahan, of Magee College, also wrote of the campaign:

His terrific severity is the faithfulness of a man who knows from experience the murderous thralldom of sin, and his motherlike tenderness is the love born at the cross where God's Son redeems sinful men. In the course of this six-week mission, three on the east and three on the west side of the Foyle, about 1,500 have come into the enquiry room seeking to learn the way of life and peace. In truth he has been a liberating force to vast numbers who have too much associated religion with outward dignity and decorum instead of peace and joy; and for long days to come the voice of gladness and rejoicing will put to shame all the empty follies of Vanity Fair.

Chapter Eleven

A Faithful Ambassador of the Cross

Belfast: After the summer holidays William returned to the Sandy Row district of Belfast to commence a mission in the large hall of the Cripples' Institute. Archibald Irwin, appointed honorary secretary for the United Mission, wrote his account:

The mission was planned to cover four weeks, but the crowds coming nightly were so great and the evidences of the working of the Spirit so manifest, that it was decided to continue the mission for a further two weeks. Although it was held in the large hall of the Cripples' Institute, it was not a Cripples' Institute mission. Practically every church and mission hall in the Sandy Row area joined in the effort. Over four hundred passed through the enquiry rooms; their names and addresses were passed on by me to the ministers and missionaries of the churches and halls which those dealt with had stated they were connected with. During the entire mission standing room was at a premium. Mr. Nicholson, being an Ulsterman himself, appealed to an Ulster audience. He did not mince matters but struck out right and left at sin in every shape and form whether in professed saint or open sinner, in the church or the world. He preached salvation by faith in Jesus and sanctification by the indwelling Spirit. He may have said things of churches and individuals which would have been better left unsaid, but when all this is taken as granted, the fact remains that the Rev. W. P. Nicholson was a power for good in Ulster, and the evidences of his work for God remain.

In the month of October another mission was held in the historic Rosemary Street Presbyterian Church. One of the past ministers of this congregation was the Rev. William Gibson who wrote the authentic account of the 1859 revival, *The Year of Grace*. Again large crowds attended the meetings, and numerous decisions for Christ were made by both young and old.

St. Enochs: William held another outstanding mission in the city of Belfast in St. Enochs Presbyterian Church which was the largest Presbyterian Church building on the European side of the Atlantic. The visit of the American evangelist D. L. Moody along with his song leader Ira D. Sankey to St. Enochs and other churches did much to rekindle the revival fires of the 1859 awakening. A reporter of the Telegraph wrote the following account of his visit to the United Mission at St. Enochs which I quote in full so that we might recapture something of what it must have been like to be present at a Nicholson United Mission.

"HEN FOOTED RELIGION" - MR. NICHOLSON'S FULL BLOODED ADDRESS

St. Enoch's is packed every night from floor to ceiling, even the pulpit is crammed with people and the choir alcove filled to the full at the mission being conducted by the Rev. W. P. Nicholson. Announced to commence at eight the church is packed at six in the ordinary sense that every seat the builder provided has almost two people on it, and by seven o'clock every inch which will accommodate a worshiper is taken up. When a *Telegraph* man went there at 6:45—the opening of the second week of the mission—there was no room on the ground floor save a little space tight against the pulpit. That great house seemed to sway with singing. Chorus followed chorus, and one was broken up by loud applause as the missioner came to the pulpit at five minutes past seven. He announced a hymn and listened to the singing.

"It reminds me," he interjected, "of Paddy in the high-class restaurant who had all the courses and then said, 'Your samples were good, but bring my dinner now.'"

"Get your nose wiped ma'am," he counselled, "and get your glasses on. You bald headed fellows get ready."

Then the women were asked to sing, "It's far better to get them singing than growling at you. What do you say, men?" A deep chorus of "Yes" came from the galleries.

Whistling and "double-barrelled solo singing" followed with the missioner's advice, "You have looked solemn long enough. Try doing something desperate. Try whistling it, and God will forgive you."

The married ladies present were invited to sing. "Don't be ashamed you are married," said Mr. Nicholson. "You may be ashamed of the thing you married, but don't be ashamed you're married."

After the "independent ladies" had sung, the entire congregation joined, Mr. Nicholson urging, "Pull out the stops and give her beans this time."

WASHBOARD-MANICURED NAILS

"Those who manicured their nails on the washboard today" sang next, and it seemed to have been the close of washing day for a big company.

The tuneful mission chorus *Joy Bells Ringing in My Soul Today* was followed by one with a sort of kick in it, having as the last three words, "Saved, saved, saved."

"That," said the missioner, "is a word the Pharisees hate, and the devil, and the old holy bachelors. Sing it out so that they will hear it down Rosemary Street. They need it very badly down there."

Rev. Nicholson next read a portion of St. John 14, beginning, "And I will pray the Father, and He will give you another Comforter," after which the Rev. Corkey led in prayer.

Announcing that he had got his hair cut that day, the missioner parodied, "From long-haired men and short-haired women good Lord deliver us." There is always," he went on, "a want about a woman with short hair and petticoats. Those old bobbed-tailed things. Never marry one of them, boys. The glory of a woman is in her hair, and the devil likes to get it cut off you."

Announcing that Friday night would be prohibition night, Mr. Nicholson said, "Prohibition, but none of your compensation. If anything gets me mad it's compensation. The dirty bloodsuckers, to compensate them! Get the stuff to hell where it belongs!" From the gallery reserved for working men came a long roar of applause.

A CHRISTIAN IN HELL

"If you show me," he went on, "a Christian brewer or distiller, I will show you a Christian in hell, and I could not do it. Curse of God on it. It is blood money. (Cries of 'Hear, hear') The North Belfast Temperance Council, or whatever you call it, have a resolution to put before you on Friday night. I will have more than a resolution for them. I always feel I am growing in grace when I am lambasting that God-cursed traffic. On Friday night I am going to speak on 'The Public-house, the Human Slaughterhouse.' If you are anything delicate about the lugs, stay at home. I have been a kind o' decent for two weeks, moderate and careful how I got on, but on Friday night!"

The speaker closed with a shrill whistle which was drowned in thunders of applause. "May God grant that you and I will live to see the day when Ulster is done dry. Every church will be open that day as in America, and bedraggled wives and hungry children will go in and thank God the day has come, but the brewers and distillers will be mad. They were mad in America, and have not got over it yet."

After a hymn came the address founded on the verses previously read. Speaking of emotional religion, the missioner declared that the reception of the Holy Ghost did not mean spasms up the back or a creeping feeling. It did not depend on anything like that. He believed there was emotion in genuine religion, for the fruit of the spirit is joy, love, peace.

UNBLOODY UNITARIANS

"Every man born into the world is unique. There had never been one like him exactly, and never would be one like him again. When God created you and me He broke the mould, and we are unique through all eternity. You will say thank God for that. It would be terrible to have two fellows like me in Ulster. I wonder what some of the ministers would do? What would the unbloody Unitarians do? What would the dirty blood sucking publicans do if there were about a hundred like me? Why then should I put myself in Paul's harness? I do not talk like you. I do not think the way you do. There is something peculiar to every one of us. Why should I try to put myself in your skin?

"Some people always believed what people told them. They took skimmed milk and neglected the cow. The Bible is your cow. Do not heed what any man tells you.

"Some fool wrote in the newspapers objecting to me talking about Christ as if He was my next door neighbour. He is far nearer to me than my next door neighbour. He is in my heart.

"To saved men the Bible from Genesis to Revelation was the Word of God, but to the unbloody Unitarians it contained the Word.

"Ma'am, when you were manicuring your nails on the washboard today how many things did you think of? You did not know whether you were washing or in heaven. If you are living as half-baked and half-boiled believers live, you have not that experience.

"My Bible says I have mansions in the sky, and I am so sure the title deeds are right that I feel I am already in possession.

"'People sing 'There's a Friend for little children above the bright blue sky,' and that sky is ninety-three million miles away, and there's a 'Friend' above that."

FIGHTING THE DEVIL ON
THE SHANKILL

"If you were fighting the devil on the Shankill Road and the Friend was ninety-three million miles away, He could not do you much good. He could have the rags off your back before help came.

"In twenty-three years I never had a conscious hour when I was unconscious of a present Saviour. I am more familiar with Jesus Christ than I am with my wife. I know the Lord far more intimately than I know my old mother. God bless you, we are just chums together. I have not got a bother, or care, or trouble, or joy, or drop of blood or one penny that is not His.

"No wonder some of you pull faces like a tombstone or an old donkey and come here to meet with the Lord, and you have not met him all week.

"There are people who have a Jesus who lived 2,000 years ago and is now in heaven far, farr, farrr away. Thank God, Christ is near.

"If some curates asked in their pulpit voice for a plate of porridge in the morning the wife would hit them with the pot.

"No unbloody Unitarian will be in heaven, who has denied the death of Christ. On that day you will kneel down and confess. Every damned spirit and the old devil and every church of God, angel and archangel, will bow the knee and confess the Lordship of Jesus.

"An old coloured believer once prayed, 'Give me a hen-footed religion.' An elder asked, 'What is a hen-footed religion?' 'One that can't walk backwards,' said the negro.'"

FIGHT, YOU SUCKER; FIGHT

He advised the men not to desert their religion, and if they did go down, to sink with the flag up! "The Lord saved you to make you a soldier. Fight, you sucker you, fight." Some there were that just the crack of a gun and the smell of powder would summon them amongst the militia on the way home. "If you are a Presbyterian and an elder, you are foreordained and they can't put you out, but if you are a Methodist, God pity you."

"A minister came to me and said, 'Could you not be a bit easier? Why, God's church is going into pieces. Couldn't you modify things a bit and let us have peace?' I said there is something worse than a row and a split. It is a false peace. When you have got billy goats amongst the sheep, the horns get clashing. It's a healthy sign to find the goats fighting.

"They had a lot of sugar candy Christianity. They had a football club for the boys, a whist drive for the old maids, a daffodil tea for the grandmothers, and then you have a jumble sale to get rid of your old rags and give them to poor God."

The speaker concluded by urging those who had decided for Christ to stand fast, never doubting, never yielding, never questioning, and it would not be long until their souls were full of the melody of heaven.

An after meeting was attended by hundreds.

An impression of the St. Enochs campaign was given by the minister, Dr. John Pollock, in the *Life of Faith*:

In response to his final appeals, over 1,500 have passed through the enquiry rooms in St. Enochs alone. This I regard as the chief excellence of Mr. Nicholson's work, that it is influencing our young men and women. He is, like myself, a strong believer in Christian endeavour; and "no wonder," he says, "for it gave me my wife." Many new societies have been formed and old ones resuscitated. One feature of Mr.

Nicholson calls for special recognition—his marvellous influence with men.

Before my ordination and during my long ministry, I have come into close contact with some of the most prominent and successful evangelists of this generation.... The opinion may seem extravagant, but I register it deliberately and without hesitation that Nicholson is second to none, if not indeed superior to all, as an expert in the divine art of winning souls.

After the St. Enoch's mission William then moved to East Belfast and conducted two other missions. The first of these was in Newtownards Road Methodist Church. It commenced in January 1923 with twenty of the neighbouring churches cooperating. The Rev. John Redmond, vicar of St. Patrick's Church, Ballymacarrett, reported, "The services gave rise to a great spiritual movement in East Belfast. Men marched in hundreds from the shipyard to the services. On one occasion so great was the pressure of men to get through the church gate that the top of one of the pillars was pushed off. In all, about four hundred of our parishioners professed conversion."

One shipyard worker was inspired to compose the following verses concerning the march.

What means the curious eager throng
That lines the streets and wait so long,
And what went ye out for to see?
The Island men in dungaree,
Those are the men that have been won
For Christ by Pastor Nicholson,
Make way, make way, you hear the cry,
And let the Islandmen pass by.

They come, they come, you hear them sing,
And loud their songs of praises ring.
Ballymacarrett is glad to see
Her sons from sin and bondage free,

While shouts and praises fill the air,
The devil leaves them in despair,
And once again you hear the cry -
The Islandmen are passing by.

No bullets fly, no bombs explode,
For Jesus leads them on the road,
Peace is proclaimed, and all is well,
The devil has lost recruits for hell.
Down in the dumps we'll let him go,
And that's the place to keep him low;
Make way, make way, you hear the cry,
And let the Islandmen pass by.

Oh, wondrous change, who can it be
That moves the city mightily?
Give God the praise, for He alone
Can melt the heart that's hard as stone.
Oh, why will you procrastinate,
Tomorrow you may be too late,
Join up, join up, why will you die,
While Christ the Lord is passing by.

The second mission in East Belfast was held in Ravenhill Presbyterian Church. There was unanimous agreement by the Kirk session in November 1922 to extend a hearty invitation to William to use the Ravenhill church as one of his centres for East Belfast. This decision led to the mission in February 1923. Here too there was a special "men's only" meeting for the shipyard workers. Led by a Salvation Army band, they marched from the shipyard straight to the church. Unfortunately when they got to the church, the gates were closed. The Rev. John Ross recorded, "when the gates were opened, the crowd was so large that the men got wedged between the pillars, and so fierce was the struggle to get in that the central pillar was moved from its place." The men were eventually allowed entrance, and that night William preached with amazing power. About halfway through the address, papers were thrown over the front of the gallery, and when Mr. Nicholson enquired what this was all about, the answer came from a notorious gambler, "These are gambling papers." That evening more than one hundred men, including the gambler, passed through the enquiry room, many of them making definite decisions for Christ. The next day one of the gambler's friends said to him, "You are a lucky fellow, the two horses you backed yesterday were winners." "Oh," said he, "no more of that for me. I was in Ravenhill Church last night, and I put all I had on One Who is always a winner—the Lord Jesus Christ." From that day on he lived an out-and-out life for Christ.

During this same mission another remarkable incident took place which William only realized as he read a letter from Messrs. Musgrave. "Dear Sir, We beg to acknowledge receipt of tools returned by one of our own men, who signs himself 'ex-worker,' and we thank you for the good influence you have used in this particular case. It will gratify you to know that we have heard of other similar cases directly attributed to your good work."

As a result of the conversions of many of the shipyard men, Harland and Wolff shipbuilders were obliged to open a large shed in which to store the tools and other items of property which had been stolen and then returned. This large storage shed became known as the "Nicholson shed."

The Witness, a Presbyterian weekly, records the following report concerning the closing days of the mission, "A great number responded to the appeal by their decision to follow Christ, and in fact, they came in shoals." What a night of rejoicing there must have been in Ravenhill at that time of mighty ingathering.

Records show that the number of persons admitted that year to the Lord's Table for the first time was 110 and the following year the total number of communicants reached 556 out of 600 families.

Ballymena: "What do you think of Nicholson?" In the early spring of 1923 this was the question on the lips of everyone in Ballymena, the next town scheduled to be visited in this great series of meetings. The mission was held in Wellington Street Presbyterian Church, and the spiritual harvest was one of abundance. At a meeting of the Kirk session of April 30, 1923, it was revealed that no fewer than 361 persons with Wellington Street connections had gone through the enquiry rooms at the Nicholson mission. Further evidence of the lasting results of the mission was to be found at the May communion, when there was an unprecedented accession to the congregational membership—a total of 110 joined by profession of faith.

Some can still recall the singing of the shipyard men as they marched in procession through the streets of Ballymena from the railway station to the Wellington Street church still wearing their working clothes and many of them carrying paraffin lamps to illuminate the pages of their Alexander hymn books.

On the last night of the mission, William was carried around the town of Ballymena on the shoulders of the shipyard men. The mission was not only a wonderful time of blessing for the church and community, but an unforgettable experience for the evangelist. Over 2,530 persons, young and old, passed through the enquiry rooms to receive Christ as their Saviour.

Carrickfergus: The final mission of the series took place in the First Church of Carrickfergus which was the oldest Presbyterian congregation in Ireland. It was held in March under the auspice of the local branch of the Christian Workers Union. Here too there was a time of reaping when large numbers of men, women and young people said, "I will," in response to the invitation of the evangelist. In the following August, the Kirk session had the joy of receiving thirty-six new members into the church. Some of the older people said they had known nothing like it since the days of D. L. Moody.

Towards the end of June, before William and his wife left for Los Angeles, a great farewell meeting was held in the Albert Hall of the Shankill Road Mission. Dr. Henry Montgomery, chairman of the meeting, said, "God had endowed Mr. and Mrs. Nicholson with spiritual qualifications to carry on a great and good work, leading multitudes of people to know Christ and stimulating God's children to a better and more Christian life and more helpful service." All present at the farewell meeting rejoiced in Mr. Nicholson's fidelity to the Word of God and in the moral and spiritual strength of his ministry. William used no flattering phrases or honeyed expressions, and he offended many who resented the strong language he used, but he did not think any of his own language was stronger than that of Christ or John the Baptist. The language of Scripture was plain and could not be misunderstood.

William's reply to his farewell address was typical, "All would be poor satisfaction to us if we had been guilty of compromise or catering to worldliness in the church or unbelief in the pulpit or pew. We have dreaded neither the censure of enemies nor sought the smiles of friends but without fear or favour have declared the whole counsel of God. I can humbly say before God that while many things were said and done which might have been better unsaid or left undone, yet I have been true to the Word of God so far as I have known it and true to the souls and salvation of my hearers."

One of the highlights of the evening was the presentation of a beautiful engraved leather bound album with illustrations and records of many of the towns and cities in Ulster where the great missions where held. The album was signed by representatives from each mission. The text of the illuminated address was as follows:

ADDRESS TO REV. W. P. NICHOLSON

At the close of a long and very successful Evangelistic Campaign in Ulster 1921 - 1923

Dear Mr. Nicholson,

We cannot allow you to leave the shores of your native Ulster without letting you know how much tens of thousands who have profited by your faithful and untiring labours in the Gospel in many centres over this northern land admire and love you for your work's sake.

You came amongst us as a faithful ambassador of the Cross and with a good record behind you of splendid services rendered for Christ in many lands, including Australia and the United States. Now there are

PHOTOGRAPH
SECTION

The front view of the birthplace of 'W.P.'.
Cotton House, near Bangor, Co. Down.

The rear view of the birthplace of 'W.P'. Cotton House, near Bangor, Co. Down.

'W.P.' as an apprentice on the 'Galgorm Castle' 1891-6.

A Nicholson family gathering. 'W.P.' is second from the left (back row).

'W.P.' with his two brothers James and Louis.

'W.P.' with his wife and family.

Rev. Dr. Montgomery.

A donkey cart bearing the Good News. Note that the donkey is inside the box!

Conlig Orange Hall.

Bible Training Institute, Glasgow.

Assembly Hall, Belfast.

A section of the crowd at the Keswick Convention.

A section of the crowd at the Keswick Convention.

The Nicholsons in 1958.

'W.P' and Mrs. Nicholson together with Song Leader Mr. Hemminger (centre back).

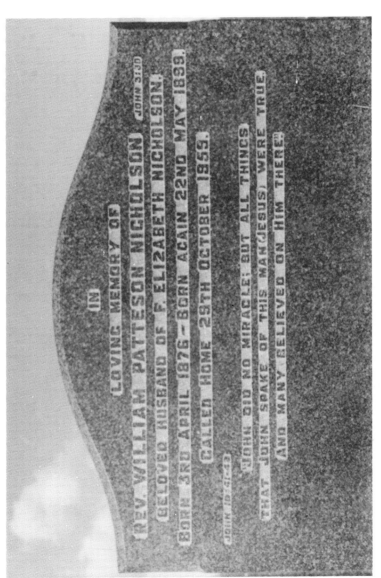

W.P. Nicholson's grave

MOODY MEMORIAL CHURCH

"Ever Welcome to this House of God are Strangers and the 'Poor'" D. L. MOODY

LOCATED BETWEEN CLARK AND LA SALLE STS. AT NORTH AVENUE

CHICAGO, ILL.

thousands in our own land who regard you with warm affection as being the honoured instrument of their salvation through faith in Jesus Christ. We believe, however, that God anointed you with a double portion of His Spirit for the great work to which He called you in Ulster.

Here in this your native province vast multitudes have waited on your ministry, which for fervour, for spirituality, for fidelity to the Word of God, for pungency of expression and for gripping speech has seldom if ever been excelled in this country.

But we specially rejoice that whilst your ministry has fallen like showers upon the parched land for Christians, it has been eminently blessed in leading thousands of men and women and young people to accept Jesus Christ as their Saviour and to enlist under His banner for His service and glory.

We recognise with warmest gratitude that you have found in Mrs. Nicholson so true a help-meet. Her services (when she was able to render them) in connection with the great campaign now closing have been as acceptable as your own. She, too, has been used of God for leading many into the light and liberty of the Gospel.

It is impossible to tabulate by mere words the deep and abiding spiritual influences that have been brought into being through your instrumentality. Ulster wears a new look today because of what God has permitted you to do amongst us. "The voice of rejoicing and salvation is in the tabernacles of the righteous: for the right hand of the Lord has done valiantly."

Whilst we thank your dear wife and yourself with all our hearts for what the Lord has enabled you do to for Him and His cause here, we give God all the glory.

It is a great delight to us to think of the new bond of loving Christian union that has been established between you and ourselves which nothing can dissolve.

You will live in the hearts of multitudes of God's redeemed people in this land so long as life and memory shall last.

Because of this bond we now invite you to return to our shores as soon as the Pillar of Cloud moves in our direction, and assure you of a very hearty welcome.

Prevented by you from offering any very tangible expression of our gratitude and affection, we beg your kind acceptance of this Album, with the names of representatives from the various centres in Ulster where your faithful and fruitful ministry has been exercised.

We remain,
Affectionately yours in Gospel fellowship,

Henry Montgomery, Chairman

E. B. Cullen	W. R. Sloan
H. Stephens Richardson	R. Nimmon
James Soye	S. G. Montgomery, Hon. Secretary
H. Livingstone Junior	Thomas Bailie, Asst. Hon. Secretary

The list of signatories to the address included ministers from the main Protestant denominations. Representatives from the Tramway Men, Shipyard Workers and Christian Workers Union Halls highlight the wide-spread support William had in the early years of his missions which in no small measure contributed to the success of his campaigns.

The meeting ended with the Nicholson Doxology: "Down in the dumps I'll never go," and the waving of white handkerchiefs which was one of the unique features of a Nicholson mission.

Thus ended a series of missions that resulted in a revival which brought salvation to thousands, breathed new life into the churches and swept away much of the blood shed, bitter strife and horrors of the civil war that threatened the land.

A friend who corresponded with William in 1959 wrote that there was much preaching in the churches on the 1859 revival. William's reply was brief and to the point, "Brother, they could have another, and greater revival, if they would pay the price. God is as keen and as able as ever to give revival, but only on His terms." William paid the price and became a flame for God in Ulster as he humbled himself to be used as God's instrument of revival.

Chapter Twelve

CONTINUING IN REVIVAL

After a three year leave of absence from the Bible Institute of Los Angeles, William returned to North America to commence an evangelistic campaign in Los Angeles in August. Many were anxious to hear first hand of the wonderful revival experiences which had taken place during those three memorable years in Ulster.

Throughout the year, William received a number of invitations to return again to his native land to hold more evangelistic campaigns. But in fairness to the Bible Institute, he felt it would be better if he resigned from his position as an extension evangelist so that he could give himself whole heartedly to the work in Ulster and around the world.

And so, one year later in July 1924, William and his wife returned to the North of Ireland to begin a series of ten missions in many of the smaller towns across the province. This campaign also made a considerable impact on the spiritual life of the churches involved, and many people confessed Christ as Saviour .

The two most outstanding missions of the campaign were in Magherafelt and Belfast. The mission in Magherafelt was held in the

Presbyterian Church, known locally as the Upper Meeting House, under the auspices of the Christian Workers Union. Here too, there was a movement of the Spirit of God, and a large number of conversions took place. A number of young men were saved, and their interest in the things of God brought them together for Bible study and prayer. During these studies, the subject of baptism came up for discussion, and it was discovered that a number of them were considering this matter, with the result that six of them went to Tobermore Baptist church and were baptized.

These young men soon felt that they were not wanted by other Christians, and as a result of this isolation, they got together for prayer, and as they prayed they began to consider the possibility of forming a Baptist church in the town. In an old disused house which belonged to the father of one of the young men, much prayer was offered that God would open a door. One night, during a time of prayer, a dog, hearing their earnest petitions, began to bark. This attracted the attention of the owner of the house, who set out to discover the cause. He found a number of young men in prayer, among them his own son. His presence made it difficult for them to pray, especially when they were praying about the forming of a Baptist Church. After some hesitation the subject of their praying was made known to the visitor. Truly "God moves in mysterious ways" for the unexpected, and be it said unwelcome visitor, proved to be God's answer to their prayers.

Although of a different denomination, he offered to help them, and before long two fields near the town came on the market, and were purchased by him without opposition. On one of these fields Pastor McKillen placed a portable hall and he himself conducted the first week of meetings. These were continued by Pastor Carser and Pastor Burrows. On Monday night, April 8, 1926, Pastor Burrows, after preaching on the subject, "What is a New Testament Church?" asked those interested to remain behind. Thirteen remained, among them four of the six young men who were baptized in Tobermore, and on that night Magherafelt Baptist Church was born.

The mission in Belfast, which was also the last mission of the campaign, was held in the historic Assembly Hall of the Presbyterian

Church in the heart of the city. Although held in this building, the mission was arranged by an interdenominational committee, which represented most of the denominations of the City of Belfast. Many expressed concern as to the timing of the mission, as August was a holiday month and a large section of the population would be away on holiday. But William was convinced of the Lord's will that the mission should proceed.

The meetings began on Sunday 2nd August, 1925. The afternoon service was to commence at 2.30 p.m. but long before that the Assembly Hall was crowded out with over 3,000 in attendance. The evening meeting was due to begin at 8.15 p.m. and again the Hall was packed long before that time.

During the course of the mission hundreds stood and said, "I will," to Christ and came to know Him as Saviour and Lord.

A few young men who were training to be missionaries, were invited to meet William and to give a five minute testimony. One of these young men was Joe Wright, whose brother Fred, along with two of his companions, had been killed by the Indians in Brazil. Joe, and his friends were awaiting the arrival of William in an ante room, when suddenly the door burst open and he entered the room like a tornado. One small Presbyterian minister, in a jovial manner, greeted him by confronting him with his fists up like a boxer. "Get out of my way, I've eaten bigger things for my breakfast," said William, with a wave of his right arm.

Some of the young men, who were from London, were shaken by what they had witnessed. One of them asked, "Is he the Rev. W. P. Nicholson?" "Yes," replied Joe.

Whatever the first impressions these young visitors had about William, they were soon dispelled as they saw a congregation of 3,000 people held captive for a solid hour as this "brand from the burning" preached with divine unction and scores of men and women leave their seats for the enquiry rooms. It was an unforgettable experience for Joe and his friends.

A final report of the Mission was given in the *Witness*, a Presbyterian weekly: "The attendance has been phenomenal, surpassing all the expectations of the promoters and committee." So great was the desire to find accommodation that the hall, which is the most spacious in the city, could on some occasions have been filled twice over.

The closing moments of the mission can never be forgotten, when the evangelist himself, visibly moved by the solemnity of the occasion, made his last appeal to the halting who up to that time had remained unmoved. Men and women quietly and deliberately, took the all important step and walked into the enquiry room and registered their decision."

Chapter Thirteen

SOUTH OF THE BORDER

It was in November, 1925 that William crossed the border to conduct a mission in the Metropolitan Hall in Dublin, under the auspices of the City of Dublin Y.M.C.A. This great hall had been erected in 1880, and D. L. Moody had given a personal subscription of one thousand dollars towards the cost of its construction.

One of the leaders in Dublin at that time, Captain Reginald Wallis, threw himself wholeheartedly into the work of the gospel campaign conducted by William. In his estimate, "Mr. Nicholson is unquestionably one of the most powerful evangelists in the Master's vineyard today. His vocabulary is certainly strange and unusual, and his methods of presenting the truth are peculiarly his own. His message has a true Scriptural ring about it and teeth that bite to the very bone. Many of us are praising God for raising up such a stalwart for the truth. His ministry flows from a heart burning in love for his Lord and Master and a deep passion for souls born from above."

The Rev. T. C. Hammond, Superintendent of the Irish Church Missions and a strong defender of Evangelical Protestantism, gave his support to the Nicholson mission. When William first arrived in Dublin, he was attacked by those who did not like his crude language and blunt approach. In the *Church of Ireland Gazette*, December 4, 1925, the Rev. Hammond wrote in his defence: "Those who criticize Nicholson, know little of how working men communicate. Do they suppose the truth of Christianity always requires genteel drawing room talk?"

He also wrote an appreciation of William's ministry in a further report in the Gazette.

Moody, Spurgeon and now Nicholson have been pilloried in the public press. The *unco guid* have gnashed their teeth, and Boreas has come out with a snorting Nor'easter. "He is course; he is vulgar; he is awful." Most of his critics have never heard him. None of them know him. Nicholson has the power. Watch the audience when he gets into the stride of a great subject. See the rapid alternation as the flitting emotions find expression in their faces. Now the laugh that so jars the funereally respectable. Now the strained expectancy as he leads them step by step in thought to a fitting denouement. Again the soft sigh of released tension when a period of dramatic vividness comes to a close. This is no idle buffoonery. Here at all events is a man who out of the well of human experience draws deep draughts. It will surprise and astonish the critics, but we believe that Nicholson is full of the Holy Ghost.

"But he is vulgar." So was Elijah when he taunted the prophets of Baal. So was Ezekiel when he rebuked the Israel of his day. His picture of the neglected child is not set for the drawing room. Prophets are men of direct speech. Nicholson has gone down into the depths. He knows the strange stirrings of primitive emotions. And he speaks the language of the man he wants to reach.

And look at the graphic power behind the realism of the man. We have accompanied him under a tropical moon in the shades of an African forest as he paced to and fro crying, "O God, if I could forget." We have sat with the nameless and homeless men of the mining camp who sobbed as if their hearts would break because a mulatto girl sang, "Your mother still prays for you, Jack." We have seen the storm gather on the mountain and the little burn that kissed the land into fertility suddenly transformed into a raging torrent. We have heard the grinding of the brakes as the express came to a sudden pause before the broken bridge and the wild cry of the Highland lad who flung himself before it that, by his life, he might bring that pause and save the sleeping passengers. Then we have gazed with a new and reverential awe on the thorn-crowned Sufferer who went to death for us. The man who can make earth and air and sea speak to us of the undying love of Calvary has something beside vulgarity. He knows men, but in the sublime moments of his great speeches, he persuades men that he knows God.

We have the heart-searching concerning restitution, forgiveness, witness, service, and never once the flag lowered. Never once was the gate opened to admit a single enemy of right, truth and love. With passionate pleading this man who had been snatched as a brand from the burning begged us, entreating even with tears, that God and God only should be all in all in our lives. And there have been gracious answers in Christians possessed with a new vitality, who will yet tender signal service to the Most High.

And he scorches and blisters and sears the smug hypocrites. He withers with scorn the brain proud word-spinners. He lets his fierce indignation burn against the problem-setters who speculate on a fallen humanity and leave the soul they have psychologised to perish. And ever there rises to his lips the great cry: "O God, may we never grow used to hearing the thud of Christless feet on the road to hell."

One of the most outstanding converts of this mission was Johnnie Cochrane, who became a Y.M.C.A. evangelist, and following the tradi-tion of his spiritual father, the Rev. W. P. Nicholson, he blazed his own trail of evangelism across Ireland and won for himself the title of "Prince of Open Air Preachers."

An account of his conversion is recorded in the *Gospel Beacon*:

In November, 1925, the Rev. William P. Nicholson came to Dub-lin to conduct a five-week Evangelistic Mission in the Metropolitan Hall (Y.M.C.A.).

It was during this mission that I was converted. Before that time I had been in touch with the Y.M.C.A. off and on for many years, but never gave any serious thought to conversion. My family was far from being religious; in fact, for years on end we would never darken a church door. We were all given to drink, and in our home it was not uncommon to sit up all night gambling and drinking so far as our means would permit.

I was much encouraged to attend this mission by my sister who came home one night and said something like the woman at the well of Samaria: "I heard a man in the Y.M.C.A. tonight, who told me more about myself than ever I knew before." Boys oh! that surely frightened me, for I thought if this fellow, whoever he was, could tell her things about herself, God only knew what he could tell about me! I was in a deplorable state, both in mind and circumstances. I was over £50 in debt for drink and had neither a rag on my back worth talking about nor a boot on my foot. Everything I could call my own, or anything to which I could lay claim, was in a pawnshop, and I had been in the hands of the police more than once. I was truly a disgrace to my name, my home, my church, and to all belonging to me. I did not know what would be the end.

At the time of this incident, I was sitting in my impoverished home with a friend, raking in the ashes for a cigarette-end which I might possibly have thrown away earlier, and wondering, wishing and talking about how we could extricate ourselves from this self-made mess in which we found ourselves.

Time and space forbid more just now, except to say that not only was I converted at this mission, but so were my father and sisters who are in Glory now and also two of my brothers. Under God, our family owes much more than can ever be expressed to dear, beloved Mr. Nicholson.

Our home was completely transformed. Instead of card playing, gambling, drinking and cursing, we had a prayer meeting every Saturday night, and this continued for over eight years in our room at the top of a five-story tenement house. The neighbours used to gather on the stairs and landing to hear the singing and listen to the preaching. We often had thirty or forty and even fifty for that weekly prayer meeting. We also held an open-air meeting every Tuesday night, just around the corner from our house.

As a result of the five-week mission, many were converted to Christ. Many decisions were made by young and old. Both Protestants and Roman Catholics together found the Saviour, and the work of the Y.M.C.A. and various churches experienced a breath of revival such as they had never known before.

Chapter Fourteen

KESWICK JUBILEE YEAR 1925

The first Keswick Convention took place in 1875 in the Lake District of Northern England. Canon T. D. Harford Battersby, vicar of the Anglican Church in Keswick, held the first convention in the grounds of his church where the meetings lasted for one week. The majority of Keswick speakers have come from all parts of the British Isles. Men such as Bishop Taylor Smith, Dr. W. Graham Scroggie, Dr. F. B. Meyer, Hudson Taylor and a host of others have preached at the Keswick Conventions. Many others such as Dr. R. A. Torrey, Donald G. Barnhouse, Archbishop Marcus Loane, and Dr. Arthur T. Pierson came from many other parts of the world.

From the beginning, the convention had for its aim, the deepening of spiritual life, the proclamation of the message of victory over sin and the reality of life more abundant through the Lordship of the indwelling Holy Spirit.

In July 1925, William crossed the Irish Sea to England to speak at the Golden Jubilee of the convention. William was scheduled to speak at the two Sunday evening evangelistic meetings; these meetings were held in the Erskine Street tent which seated 2,250. On the first Sunday evening, the crowds gathered into the tent to hear this rough and ready Irish evangelist who had been so mightily used of God in the North of Ireland, and soon it was filled to capacity. William's sermon was based upon the Biblical story of Philippian jailer and his question, "What must I do to be saved?" William related to his audience how one Sunday evening after he had preached in the open air in Bangor, he put his hand on the shoulder of a man who had seemed to be deeply interested during the service. "I said, 'Well are you a saved man?' 'Leave me alone,' he replied, 'I am sick to death with you preachers.' 'That's not answering my question,' I said. 'Well,' said the man, 'you might come along the shore, and we will talk things over.'"

As they walked along Bangor's cold shore, William learned that the young man had originally come from Bangor and had gone out to Canada with his parents when he was still a little child. He had also been an elder for thirty-three years in a Presbyterian church. The man continued, "I have heard sermons all my life on salvation, the joy of salvation, and the power and blessing of salvation; many times I have been urged to receive salvation because it would be necessary not only for my present good but also for my eternal welfare. Well, let me say that I have never heard any minister telling me how to get what I ought to have."

Nicholson admitted to his audience, "I could have hung my head in shame. Because we live in a Christian country, we expect that everybody is familiar with the way in which to be saved. I want to make it as clear as I can to everyone here tonight. You may not like what I say, but I guarantee you will understand every word before I am done. It is a very short time 'til the place that knows us will know us no more forever. God only knows how soon some of us will be in the presence of the King, and if you are not saved tonight you may be in hell as long as God lives."

Simply, yet powerfully, Nicholson explained God's way of salvation, and when he made his appeal, many responded to the invitation to receive Christ.

The tent meetings were great, but meetings were also held in the open air. William shared these open-airs with the Scottish veteran, Rev. John McNeill; both were rough hewn men of common stock, and each had the power to have the crowds laughing uproariously one moment and intensely solemn the next. Other Christians were also asked to testify to the saving power of Christ. Officers in the Navy and Army and professional men from all walks of life took part. These open-airs attracted large crowds and were greatly blessed by God.

The various universities, including Oxford and Cambridge, sent their representatives to the convention. Bishop Taylor Smith and others were invited to speak to the students at some of the university houses. One evening William was also invited. He was reluctant at first to accept the invitation; he knew that he could not meet them on scholastic grounds, but he finally decided to go, and they treated him with courtesy and gave to him their full attention.

The next morning when he went to meet J. Kennedy Maclean, William was bubbling over with a holy joy. He told how he had been with the university students until 2:00 a.m. and how between twenty and thirty students had got down on their knees before God and surrendered their lives to the Lord.

William's message on the final Sunday night was again held in the Erskine Street tent. He preached from the text in Genesis 6:3, "And the Lord said, My Spirit shall not always strive with man." He claimed that this text was instrumental in bringing him to Jesus Christ as his personal Saviour. He recalled how "sweat started on my brow; the veins stood up as thick as my finger; the fear of God fell upon me; the very pains of Hell took hold of me; the very sorrows of the damned seemed to grip me, and in anguish and in agony I knew I was up against my destiny that morning as if God had said to me, 'Now or Never!' I believe that when the books are opened yonder I will find that the 22nd day of May, 1899, is the day when I would have crossed the boundary line between God's patience and God's wrath if I had rejected Jesus Christ, but, thank God, that Monday morning I accepted Him as my Saviour."

At the close of this very powerful message William made his final appeal, and once again all over the tent there were those who stood to their feet and cried, "I will," and surrendered their lives to Christ.

Dr. W. Graham Scroggie remarked of that week, "They may say what they like about Nicholson, but after all, the test of a man's work and words is the goods he delivers—and he has delivered the goods."

Many remember that the weather was very pleasant throughout the whole week, but best of all, the "Sun of Righteousness had risen with healing in his wings," and the Lord richly blessed all those present.

Chapter Fifteen

"WILLIE NICK" AT CAMBRIDGE

The established custom of the Cambridge Inter-Collegiate Christian Union (always known as C.I.C.C.U.) was to hold a mission in Cambridge every three years. The Lent term was chosen, and three speakers of varying outlook and religious experience were invited as the missioners.

Three men were chosen for the United Mission of 1926; they were the Bishop of Manchester, William Temple, Dr. F. W. Norwood of the City Temple and Dr. Stuart Holden. Dr. Holden suggested to the committee that they should invite William to come for three days of mission preparation, to stir up the C.I.C.C.U to prayer and service.

Dr. Basil Atkinson, an under-librarian at the university, was unhappy with the choice of Stuart Holden who had made statements, especially in America, which had upset many and worried those who loved and admired him. Atkinson was so concerned, he began to pray that Holden would not come. A week before the mission was to commence, word was received that Stuart Holden had withdrawn on the grounds of ill health. There was dismay among the leaders of the C.I.C.C.U., because suitable speakers were few and hard to find, and the committee was unable to think of anyone who would be free at such short notice.

Harold Earnshaw-Smith, who had been to the C.I.C.C.U. camp at Keswick that summer, had been greatly impressed with William Nicholson (Willie Nick as the students called him), and the committee decided in the end to ask William to replace Stuart Holden as the Missioner. The contrast between Holden and William could not have been greater. Holden had a charming personality; he was gracious and winsome, highly musical and a brilliant speaker. William was rough and rude, and had no fear of men. He was extremely blunt and hard hitting about sin, repentance and hell.

A group of students went to Euston Station to meet him, and as soon as he had stepped off the train they suggested that he take Holden's place. William said afterwards, "I nearly fainted. I would rather have entered a den of lions." "I can't talk to University men," was his reply. "I'm just a simple sailor fellow, but let's have a word of prayer." So they prayed there and then on the Euston station platform, and William threw his hat in the air and shouted, "Praise the Lord!"

The three days of preparatory talks for which William had originally come soon revealed what sort of person and preacher he was. J. B. Tupman of Corpus wrote, concerning the outcome of these talks, "We were faced with our responsibilities to our fellow students who were without Christ; the meetings were searching times." It was impossible for the men to remain complacent under William. "There are so few clean and strong hands prepared unto every good work, especially lifting men to Christ. This is the work that counts most. The one business of the Devil is to damn. The one business of the Lord is to save. Both are busy at this all the time. We never succeed by the compromise. We can never win men to Christ until we show them we have something far better than they have and that we are enjoying it." But he then went on to shock the students, "Why are you fellows wearing those black things on your backs?" He was referring to their academic gowns. "Why don't you pawn them and go and buy Bibles?" In spite of William's strong language and straight-from-the-shoulder preaching, the students warmed to his forthright manner and gave him their whole hearted support.

The mission commenced on Saturday, January 31, with a united meeting in the Guildhall. The president of the Union Society, Michael Ramsey, who afterwards became the 100th Archbishop of Canterbury, took the chair. The hall was packed, and Ramsey read the opening prayers; he then spoke to his fellow undergraduates about their attitude to the mission, warning them that if they felt critical, to beware lest they be found to be fighting against God.

Bishop William Temple was the first speaker, and he was followed by Dr. F. W. Norwood. The chairman then announced Stuart Holden's withdrawal and called upon William to speak.

"I understand" began William, "that the purpose of this gathering is to introduce the missioners to you. My Lord Bishop is well known, and so is Dr. Norwood. But I am an unknown quantity. Who am I?" And with a voice like a bull he went on, "My name is William P. Nicholson of Bangor, County Down, Northern Ireland. I was born on 3rd April, 1876, I was born again on 22nd May 1898, and I was filled with the Spirit in November 1898 through the ministry of Dr. Stuart Holden of London. And what do I believe? I believe in God the Father Almighty, maker of heaven and earth, and in Jesus Christ His only Son our Lord. I believe He was conceived by the Holy Ghost. I believe He was born of the Virgin Mary, yes, born of the Virgin Mary..." As he continued reciting the Aposles' Creed he came to the phrase "From whence also He shall come again to judge both the quick and the dead," and as he spoke of the literal second coming of Christ, many in the room laughed. When he came to the end of the Apostles' Creed, "I believe in the Life everlasting—yes, the eternity of Hell and the eternity of Heaven," he said, "That's me, and that's my message," and he promptly sat down in his seat.

The students were astounded, and Michael Ramsey could only rise and announce the closing hymn. Afterwards Dr. Norwood snubbed William by deliberately turning his back on him, but Bishop Temple took him by the hand and wished him God-speed.

Harold Earnshaw-Smith, who was rather annoyed with William, said, "Whatever made you do that? Now you've ruined everything."

William replied, "Brother Smith, if I had done what you thought, and pleased everybody, it would have been the end of your mission. Now you'll see. God will work."

William's opening meeting was held in Holy Trinity Church, and the congregation was no larger than on a normal Sunday evening. Most of the students had flocked to Great St. Mary's to hear William Temple. Nicholson was so conscious of his inferiority that he was amazed and encouraged to see so many. He preached for a full hour on the text "Ye must be born again." And there was no watering down of the message. He was not preaching to students but to sinners who needed the experience of the new birth. "If Jesus only came to this world to be an example of a perfect human life and a teacher, He has only come to mock poor, helpless, ruined humanity in its helpless, hopeless condition... Christianity is not merely a perfected life presented but is essentially and supremely a divine life communicated. Ye must be born again if you would enter the kingdom of heaven. There is no subject so unpopular in the world today as this—Ye must be born again."

One of the students who had been taken along by a friend to hear William was heard to say, "It was extraordinary, very vulgar and yet very attractive at the same time."

At the end of his message William made an appeal for any who would accept Christ as their personal Saviour to stand up. "Is there a man here who has the courage of his convictions? Will you stand up and say 'Yes sir, I will.' No eyes closed or any of this hokey-pokey business of heads bowed, but just stand up and say 'I will.'"

There were about ten men who stood up, and they were asked to come forward to the front. When the service was over they were taken by Earnshaw-Smith to the Henry Martyn Hall, and there they were counselled by assistant missioners who pointed them to Christ.

The news of William's first sermon spread around the university like wildfire. Attendance at his meetings increased, although some came merely out of curiosity. One man wrote, "There was never a dull or conventional moment; you never knew what he would say next!"

The students were encouraged to invite William to their rooms for meals. Two such students were K. J. Dallison and Stafford Wright (who later became Principal of Tyndale Hall). Mr. Dallison wrote, "We invited him to breakfast, and he told us how much he enjoyed his visit. So many of the students were ex-public school boys, and it was a relief for him to be among 'secondary school types' once again. He shared with us his nervousness at the thought of his coming to Cambridge, and how his mother had strengthened him by reminding him that 'God shut the lions mouths for Daniel, and He would do similar for him.'"

Many stories of "Willie Nick" and his preaching were soon doing the rounds. One is told of when he preached on the text "The hairs of your head are all numbered;" he pointed at a bald-headed man in the audience and remarked, "The Lord wouldna take long over you!" Another is told of how, after a story of an aunt of his who had died unregenerate and had gone to hell; he saw two men leaving the church, and shouted, "If you leave this church unsaved, you too will go to hell!" and one of the men shouted back, the remark being nearly lost in the roar of laughter which followed, "Any message for your aunt?"

Each night many more men came to hear William than went to hear Norwood and Temple. Among them was Michael Ramsey, who having attended Holy Trinity Church as a child decided that he had better go and hear for himself this fiery preacher from Northern Ireland. "As I went in he was getting very worked up. Very worked up indeed. He was using very foul language. And there were a couple of rather rough chaps from Magdalene, whom I knew, sitting in front of me, crying. This surprised me a great deal. After singing a hymn, this evangelical preacher said, 'Now hypocrites, go back to your women and cigarettes.' I thought to myself, well, I haven't got a girlfriend, and I don't smoke so I can stay. After another verse of the hymn the preacher said, 'All those who wish to declare, stand up.' And all around me, it was very alarming, people were jumping up, and I thought I might be impelled to do so by mistake!"

Harold Earnshaw-Smith along with other members of the C.I.C.C.U. were now seeing the fulfillment of William's words which he had spoken that night at the Guildhall, "Now you'll see, God will work."

God worked in the lives of men who had before been only nominal Christians. One in particular was the president of the Drunk's Club. This man stood at William's appeal and came back the next night with friends who would not have come on their own. These friends subsequently brought others with them the following night, and many of them came to know the Lord as their Saviour.

On the last weekend of the mission there was no meeting planned for Saturday night, but the committee decided that William should speak that evening at Holy Trinity, and it was filled to capacity. He spoke on the text "Almost persuaded," and at the close of his message he made his usual appeal. But for the first time that week no-one responded. William leaned back in the pulpit. "I know what is wrong with this meeting tonight. There are too many hypocrites in the church! Too many blue-eyed, hatchet-faced, lily-livered hypocrites! While we sing the first verse of the next hymn, will the hypocrites please leave the church." During the singing thirty or forty left the church, many in evident annoyance. One of them was a college chaplain who wrote the next day to the president, complaining that he had been called a hypocrite.

Still there was no response to his appeal. When the meeting was over the C.I.C.C.U. leaders and William assembled for prayer in Earnshaw-Smith's room, and there the Spirit of prayer was poured upon them.

The next morning a man went to call William for breakfast and found him on his knees, "tired and exhausted after a night of prayer." Although exhausted, William and others prayed on through the morning.

On that final Sunday night the church was again full, and William preached on the text which had been used to lead him to Christ, "My Spirit shall not always strive with man." At the end of this message over twenty-five men decided for Christ. This was more than on any of the previous nights.

The next morning there was a Thanksgiving service of Holy Communion in King's College Chapel, and nearly seven hundred communicants attended. Afterwards the Christian Union men met to say goodbye to Willie Nick. "The send off they gave me warmed my heart and humbled me," he wrote. They crowded round the motor that was taking me to London, and sang and shouted. I could hardly see for tears running down my cheeks."

The minute book of the Union records the gratitude of the General Committee. They expressed their feelings in the words of Psalm 126: "When the Lord turned again the captivity of Sion, we were like them that dream. Then was our mouth filled with laughter, and our tongue with singing... The Lord hath done great things for us; whereof we are glad."

A former president, Bishop Gough, wrote, "Nicholson's mission produced in the C.I.C.C.U. a generation through which God did certainly work. The effect on the lives of members was indelible."

Chapter Sixteen

THROUGH SUNSHINE AND SHADOW IN AUSTRALIA

Towards the end of March 1926, William, his wife and family left Ulster for their home in Los Angeles, and after a short holiday they sailed for Australia in June to begin a series of campaigns in Sydney.

Seventeen years had passed since William had been there with Dr. Wilbur Chapman and Mr. Charles Alexander. He was no longer a novice but a seasoned campaigner in the field of evangelism.

As the R.M.S. Tahiti tied up at the wharf, the Rev. R. Hammond and Mr. W. Bradley, the organizing secretary of the campaign were there to meet William. The Rev. Hammond described the meeting: "Mr. Bradley and I hurried on board to welcome W. P. Nicholson, but he had slipped off by the luggage gangway and was grinning at us from the wharf. This is characteristic of the man. He does not wait for things to happen; he makes them happen. It was a perfect day, and this big-hearted, simple, downright, stake-all-on-the-Word-of-God man landed with his wife, two daughters and son, under the happiest conditions."

On his arrival, William lost no time in getting to work. On Sunday, June 12, he addressed audiences in three different churches. This was followed by a meeting for ministers on Monday at which more than two hundred were present.

Wednesday, June 16, also proved a busy day for the evangelist. The Rev. Hammond writes concerning that day:

The most wonderful meeting in Australia, held every Wednesday in the basement of the Sydney Town Hall, was never greater than on Wednesday, 16th June. Seventeen hundred people were present between one and two o'clock. Mr. Nicholson's message was based on the text, "And whatsoever ye shall ask in my name, that will I do." (John 14:13) "The emphasis," he said, "is on *that*—not some other thing but the very thing you ask. God knew what He was saying and meant what He said." Hundreds hurried away to their places of business, but immediately every chair was filled again, and his message at 3 p.m. was broadcast. Following on his previous talk, he emphasized in his inimitable way the conditions attached to the *whatsoever*.

After the preliminary meetings, William commenced the first of his intended series of missions in Goulburn. The first week of this campaign was a stirring one. William was as blunt and as forthright as ever. Night after night, he preached upon carnal Christianity, his subjects included "Prayer—the Lost Art of the Church" and "Baptism of the Holy Ghost—the Need of the Church."

The Rev. Hammond recalls William's words early in the campaign.

"We Irish are never at peace unless we are fighting. There's enough Irish in the devil—the auld rascal—to make a good scrap. Glory to God, revival does start a row, and I love it with all my heart. If it's a revival from heaven, it will raise hell."

These blunt and characteristic expressions from the lips of the Rev. W. P. Nicholson have proved prophetic. The first week of the

Goulburn campaign has been a stirring one. The "Irishism" of the devil has been manifesting itself. Sure, there will be a great scrap. "Tread on the tail o' me coat" has been the Satanic invitation. Mr. Nicholson has jumped on it with both feet.

"The outcome of these heart-stirring messages was evidenced at the half-night of prayer held at the close of Friday's meeting. The Lord's people have been touched and refreshed. Already the revival has commenced. Apart from the weeks of cottage prayer meetings preceding the campaign, daily prayer meetings are held at 8 o'clock in the morning. These have been times of real intercession. On Sunday morning the room was full, and one late-comer was unable to find a spot to kneel upon. There is a wonderful spirit of expectancy. Thanks be unto God who giveth us the victory through the Lord Jesus Christ."

This, however, is only one side of the story. William's outspoken condemnation brought upon his head the wrath and anger of many. Unfair accounts of the mission appeared in the Press and this inflamed passions of hatred and bitterness. People believed the reports as gospel instead of coming to hear for themselves.

William decided that he would reply to the criticism and misrepresentations of the Press, and he took the opportunity to do so before his address at one of the meetings. Speaking with some warmth he remarked that this was the first time in his twenty-six years of ministry that he had condescended to reply to any attacks through the columns of the Press, but he considered it was so unfair and so un-British that out of consideration to those who were standing by the campaign he felt he should reply.

William intimated that if there were any present who felt uncomfortable and wished to leave, they had the opportunity to withdraw.

"Up Derry," yelled some hot-head, and up jumped a number of young men and women. "The Catholics are as good as you, Nicholson," yelled one of their number. This was the signal for an outburst of hostile demonstration. About fifty or more, mainly from the back seats, rushed out, yelling and cat-calling, hurling angry epithets at the evangelist. Pandemonium broke loose for a few minutes.

Hardly had he commenced his address than there was another interuption. A bucket of dirty smelling water was thrown from the ceiling of the theatre above the stage. It was evidently intended for the speaker but missed its mark and splashed over the piano and partly over the young lady pianist, who acted pluckily throughout.

William proceeded with his address which was completed without interruption. The police took prompt action to prevent any further demonstration and to apprehend, if possible, the perpetrator. It was subsequently discovered that a bucket had been suspended in the ceiling, and a long rope had been attached to allow someone to tip it from the ground. The outrage shocked the good feelings of the community and went a long way to placing Christians "on side" throughout the campaign.

Touching scenes marked the close of the meetings. Several of William's choruses were sung heartily, and *Down in the dumps I'll never go* was certainly the most popular. "Can't you stay another fortnight?" appealed the audience in chorus. But Nicholson knew he had to move on. The memorable campaign came to a close with the congregation singing with all fervour, *God be with you till we meet again.*

William's next stop was Lismore. William wrote about the new work: "What a glorious time we are having here. Whole families are being brought in. Every night men and women are deciding by the score. There is great joy in and around here, and also the old devil is clean mad. Hallelujah! The Pharisees are the same the world over, and always they oppose revival and persecute those who go in for it. I meet many here who came originally from various parts of Ulster. They love to hear the brogue."

William's time in Australia was fully occupied as he journeyed to various churches and centres doing the work of an evangelist. During his busy schedule William sought to have regular rest days which he could spend with his wife and family. His children looked forward to these special times together with their mother and father. On one such day, having just arrived at the seaside, William's wife became suddenly ill and collapsed into her husband's arms. Just as the doctor arrived, she gave a deep sigh and passed into the immediate presence of her Lord and Saviour. There were no sad goodbyes, no sickness and no wasting diseases. She was in the midst of sunshine and beautiful scenery one moment, and in the next she was in the land of unclouded sky where the roses never fade. Her body was brought home on Saturday night, and William preached three times on Sunday. The congregation did not know of his loss or aching heart.

The funeral service was held on Monday, and crowds of mourners came to express their love and sympathy. Many women wept openly for the one who had been their spiritual mother. They sang *The Land where the roses never fade, No Burdens Yonder* and *Loved with Everlasting Love.* William was enabled to preach to the crowd over her grave, taking as his text Revelation 21:5, "Write: for these words are true and faithful."

Their daughter Jessie, who was then 18 years of age, now had to take over the role of looking after the family.

William continued with his meetings in Australia for almost a year, conducting missions in various towns and cities, but the stress eventually proved too much for him, and he was compelled to postpone the remainder of his tour. Upon the advice of his doctor, he decided to take six months of complete rest.

After those long six months a stronger, refreshed William continued his campaign. During one of his missions he noticed a group of young women get up and leave the meeting early. William resented anyone leaving or disturbing his services, so he made inquiries as to who the young girls were. He discovered that they were young trainee nurses working in a local hospital and they had to be back at their halls of residence at a certain time. William decided that he would pay a visit to the matron of the hospital, Miss Fanny Elizabeth Collett, and ask her to give the young nurses permission to stay out later so that they could remain until the end of the service. She flatly refused his request, reminding him that she was responsible for the moral well-being of the young ladies and suggested to him that he should stop the service earlier.

As a result of this meeting, a friendship formed between William and Fanny, and this friendship developed when William was admitted as a patient in her hospital after suffering a severe heart attack during the mission.

Towards the end of his stay in hospital, William asked Fanny if she would like to take on the job of nursing him full time. This was his unique way of asking her to marry him, and having accepted his proposal, they were soon wed. Fanny's care and support as a wife and as a mother to his children meant much to William in the years which followed, and she travelled with him throughout the world, taking part in his evangelistic missions.

Chapter Seventeen

NICHOLSON AS I SAW HIM

There are many people who had the great privilege of meeting William Nicholson during their lifetime. This chapter records the personal recollections of a few.

DR. PAUL WHITE

My contacts with W. P. Nicholson were few but notable. When I was 16, (1926) I sat in a large tent listening to him preach, and he hit me with Hebrews 2:3, "How shall we escape, if we neglect so great salvation." This shook me to my roots, and as a result I came into the Kingdom.

I made it a practice of sending him a Jungle Doctor book as they came out and writing to him annually. I felt a great sense of thanks. He invariably replied, and he always finished his letter, "Yours restfully busy."

In the later 1940s, I chaired a meeting at which he spoke, during which he prayed, "O Lord let me never be smooth tongued but keep my tongue rough like a cows." As he spoke later it was clear that his prayer was answered; he had his Australian audience either rocking with laughter or sweating from his verbal surgery.

I had the temerity to tell him this in the middle of his talk, with a broad smile on my face. He whisked round with a similar smile, "Go back to the jungle for a bit," he urged, "and let me get on with my job."

REV. L. E. DEENS
Baptist Pastor

It was my privilege to meet W. P. on more than one occasion. I recall being alone with him in the vestry of St. Enoch's one night just before the meeting started. He offered prayer, and then, rising from his knees ran to the mantelpiece, broke two eggs into a tumbler and swallowed them in a single gulp! He explained to me that he knew nothing as good for lubricating the throat in preparation for the work it had to do! I also had the responsibility of preaching to him twice one Sunday when he happened to be spending a weekend in the Southern Metropolis with his wife. He often said hard things about the Baptists as he also did about his own denomination and several others, so I must confess I was surprised to see him in our congregation at the morning service, but he waited for the breaking of bread service and participated in it, and then he came back for the evening service. It was plain that as long as he found himself in a thoroughly evangelical atmosphere he was happy and didn't worry about denomination labels.

DR. IAN R. K. PAISLEY M.P. M.E.P.
Martyrs Memorial Free Presbyterian Church

On the Sunday after I was ordained to the ministry, 1st August, 1946, to my amazement, in my first morning service, W. P. Nicholson was in the back seat of the church. I was a mere stripling of twenty. I had sat at his feet as a boy in what was known as the 'Ahoghill Cathedral,' where he had preached to vast crowds of people.

I need not tell you I was nervous. After I had finished, the great preacher walked up to the front of the church. He said, "I have one prayer I want to offer for this young man. I will pray that God will give him a tongue like an old cow." And he said, "Go in, young man, to a butcher's shop and ask to see a cow's tongue. You will find it is sharper than any file. God give you such a tongue. Make this church a converting shop and make this preacher a disturber of Hell and the Devil."

J. OSWALD SAUNDERS

In one of the meetings at which I was present, Mr. Nicholson challenged any man to come to the services on five consecutive nights without yielding to the claims of Christ. Several evenings later I saw a man whom I knew go with his son to one counselling room and his wife and daughter to another. He was a ship's engineer who had led an unsavoury life, but he had a godly father who had long prayed for the conversion of his wayward son. It transpired that he had been present at the meeting when the challenge had been thrown out. Out of sheer bravado in his heart he accepted the challenge, but on the fifth night the conviction of the Spirit was so strong that he could resist no longer. It is not difficult to imagine the joy of the praying father, as well as the rejoicing in heaven over the prodigal's return.

ARCHBISHOP MARCUS LOANE

I spoke many times at Evangelical Union meetings in the thirties, forties and fifties, but one event stands out in my memory. It was in August 1935, when the E.U. held a University Mission for the first time. The Irish evangelist, W. P. Nicholson, was the missioner. The Union Hall was packed out for his first meeting on the Monday when he gave a straightforward testimony. An even larger and much more noisy crowd heard him the next day speak on the New Birth. He said that you cannot see the process, but the result of the New Birth is none the less real. Then he tried to illustrate his point with a series of rhetorical questions. "Can you see pain? Can you hear pain? Can you smell pain?" There was a chorus of YES in reply to each question, and he concluded by saying. "You're a bunch of liars!"

Nicholson fell ill overnight and was unable to take further part in the mission. There were no conversions (as far as I remember) as a result of that mission, but E.U. members were greatly strengthened in faith and boldness of witness.

REV. JAMES BEATTY

W. P. Nicholson came to my home town of Newtownards in Co. Down, and my impression of him is due to what happened there. He was invited by a small committee of the various churches, and he stayed about six weeks. He was a faithful and fearless preacher, and he would thunder the judgments of God upon sin as well as lovingly urge sinners to receive the Saviour. Sometimes his methods and style of humour were not always appreciated.

He was in complete control of the meetings; there was no choir or soloists, and he led the congregation in Alexander's hymns. Apart from the ministers who stood by him he had no other helpers except the ushers. When he told them to open the doors, they opened them, and when he told them to shut the doors, they shut them. Before he started to preach he would say, "If anybody wants to leave, go now, for if you don't I'll name you!" I wondered how he could do that, but it was easy: he would describe them by the clothes they were wearing. Nobody left!

I saw something in one of his meetings which I have not seen since. A man in front of me was deeply moved, and in the middle of the address stood up and said, "I will." Mr. Nicholson did not continue his message; led of the Spirit, he immediately said, "Who will be next?"

W. P. Nicholson did not escape criticism, but what Christian who is seeking to serve the Lord can avoid criticism? There is no doubt that he was a man of God raised up for a certain age, and I thank God upon every remembrance of him.

A. LINDSAY GLEGG

W. P. Nicholson came over to London to St. Paul's, Portman Square, for Dr. Stuart Holden, but apart from this, I think I am the only one who had been venturesome enough to invite him to conduct a mission in London. He came to us in 1928 for a special effort at Down Lodge Hall, London. He shocked a great many of my people with his rough tongue, but it was no use trying to change him. My wife and I did our best, with I'm afraid, no success, but still the people came, and many were converted. Dr. Graham Scroggie once said to me, "He is filled with vulgarity and with the Holy Spirit, and how a man can be filled with both at the same time I don't know." Neither do I.

The secret of his power was no doubt in his prayer life. He stayed at our home for ten days during the campaign, and although he was up in the morning at six o'clock, he never appeared until twelve noon. He spent the hours wrestling with God in prayer. My wife would take up his breakfast and leave it outside his bedroom door, but it was rarely taken in. By his own special request he was not disturbed by phone or visitor, however urgent.

He conducted a campaign for the students at Cambridge at the request of the Christian Union, and my wife and I went up to help. We met Willie Nicholson in his room for prayer and afterwards my wife, walking across to his bed said, "What have you been up to, your sheets are torn into shreds?" "Ah," said Willie, "I must tell them at the office about that." What had happened was that he, unconsciously, agonising in prayer, had ripped the sheets into strips with his strong hands and arms. Yes, prayer was surely the secret of his power.

Chapter Eighteen

A MONUMENT OF SOULS

S omeone once said of Sir Christopher Wren, the architect of St. Pauls Cathedral in London, "If you want to see his monument, look around you!" This could also be said of William P. Nicholson. His monument is the lives and ministries of those whom he won for Christ. He once paid a tribute to the Old Testament shipbuilder Noah when he said that Noah was God's evangelist for 120 years, and his text was always the same—Genesis 6:3, "My Spirit will not always strive with man." He pointed out that Noah never got a convert outside his own family; William then admitted that, as an evangelist, *he* could not have carried on without seeing some results.

As a result of William's missions, the number of students dedicated to the ministry doubled in some denominations, and the various missionary societies dealt with many applications from prospective candidates for the mission field. The home missions such as the Belfast City Mission, the Faith Mission, and the Christian Workers Union all received new workers because of the revival which took place through God's power upon William.

In every branch of the Christian church in Ireland, and in many other places throughout the world, you will find men and women who were influenced by the ministry of W. P. Nicholson. Let me introduce you to some of those who make up William's monument of souls.

REV. FRANCIS W. DIXON
Minister of Lansdowne Baptist Church, Bournemouth (1946-1975).

Francis Dixon met the Lord in a remarkable way. He was on holiday at Bexhill-on-Sea with a friend, and William was holding a campaign in a tin tabernacle in Bexhill at that time. Francis' landlady encouraged the two young men to go and hear him. They did, and God spoke to them through the powerful preaching of God's servant. Francis came to realise his desperate need of trusting the Lord Jesus Christ as his personal Saviour.

It was also through William's ministry that Francis first glimpsed the possibilities of a life of usefulness in the service of God. Only three days after his conversion he was reading his Bible and came across our Lord's words, "The Spirit of the Lord is upon me because He has anointed me to preach the gospel." William had emphasised that God has a plan for the lives of those He brings to faith in his Son. Francis Dixon knew from that moment God's plan for him was that he should preach the Gospel and that the Spirit was on him for this work.

While he was studying for the ministry, he frequently received a £5 note from William to help him through. It was a great encouragement to him that the one who had led him to Christ was also prepared to help him in such a practical manner.

As Francis travelled around the world preaching the Gospel, he found fruit from the labours of this man of God, and he rejoiced to be numbered among those who rise up to call him blessed.

FREDERICK B. BROWNE
London City Missioner

The night of 31st October, 1921, was the supreme moment of my life, for it was then I was reconciled to God.

As an ex-army captain I came to Ireland with one of the first contingents of Black and Tans in 1920, and after a harrowing time in the South, found myself a sergeant in the R.I.C. training "Specials" in the Newtownards Depot. At that time I was a Roman Catholic, and yet one of my friends was a Special Sergeant C——, a keen young Christian, whom I nevertheless regarded as a bit of a crank. He is now the dearest friend I have.

Towards the close of an intensive mission by the Rev. W. P. Nicholson (God bless him!) in the Strean Presbyterian Church, Newtownards, Sergeant C—— induced me to attend a service. It was the first Gospel meeting to which I had ever been. The Holy Spirit convicted me of sin, and I was one of the first to enter the enquiry room. I confess without shame that, although in uniform and before all, I broke down and wept bitterly. And I had been through Mons, the Somme, and Tipperary without a tear. Such is the power of the repentance for sin and the joy of forgiveness. I had never read a word of the Bible, but I set to work and spent hours daily searching the Scriptures. By the grace of God I became a Methodist local preacher and had the joy of winning many souls to the Saviour. Some time later, whilst stationed in Enniskillen, I heard the call to fuller service, and in October, 1924, three years after conversion, I became a preacher in my native city; I became a London City Missioner.

PASTOR JOHN PROCTOR
Emmanuel Mission, Belfast.

Christ got hold of John Proctor during a mission held in East Belfast in the Ravenhill Presbyterian Church in 1923. His interest in the mission was aroused after hearing the sound of the Salvation Army Band leading the shipyard men as they marched from the yard to the Ravenhill Church. Out of curiosity he went along to see and hear for himself what was happening, and that night he was arrested by the Holy Spirit and was suddenly and gloriously won for Christ. The next evening his sister Ellen also trusted the Saviour.

From the moment of his conversion he anxiously sought to know and do the will of God. He became pastor of the Emmanuel Hall, Roslyn Street, on October 1, 1932 and continued there until August 26, 1991.

Although he did not have the advantage of Bible School training, he was an able and gifted teacher and preacher of the Word of God, and through his 59 years of faithful ministry he had the joy of seeing hundreds of men and women won for Christ.

The same could be said of him as was said of John the Baptist, the forerunner of Christ, in John 10:41-42, "John did no miracle: but all things that John spake of this man were true. And many believed on Him there."

PASTOR WILLIAM WILSON
Grove Baptist Church

It was my privilege to be brought up in an evangelical Presbyterian atmosphere, and I can never remember a time when I did not know that I was a sinner needing a Saviour.

My parents belonged to the "old school" and insisted that church attendance and the learning of the Shorter Catechism should not be optional, but binding, and I am thankful that in the early and impressionable days of childhood I was taught the foundational facts of Ruin by the Fall, Redemption by the Blood and Regeneration by the Holy Spirit.

However, I remained in my unconverted state during those days and for years afterwards. But bless God, a day of deliverance dawned, and it pleased God who separated me from my mother's womb to call me by His grace on the evening of Friday, November 4, 1921 through the ministry of Rev. W. P. Nicholson.

Mr. Nicholson's campaigns in Ulster were all fruitful, but in few districts was there the stir that was witnessed in Newtownards. Scores were awakened and savingly converted, a number of whom are serving God at home and abroad.

On the evening of my translation from darkness unto the light, the preacher gave a characteristic, straight-from-the-shoulder message on the words of Romans 3:20, "Therefore by the deeds of the law shall no flesh be justified in His sight."

As I listened, the Holy Spirit swept away every prop from beneath me, and I realised that I must get Christ now as my very own Saviour or else perish forever. I saw that morality and respectability without Jesus Christ were of no avail. I learned that all religion, however sincere and orthodox, apart from the regenerating power of the Holy Ghost, was a subtle delusion, a miserable sham, an absolute falsehood and would damn my soul for all eternity. The powers of darkness were at work with intensified zeal, and all the forces of Hell would have kept me from then and there accepting Christ as my Saviour, but grace triumphed, and on the first seat of the gallery of the Strean Church, Newtownards, I was enabled to say from my heart, "Christ for me."

REV. WILLIAM JAMES GRIER, B.A.
Evangelical Presbyterian Church

William James Grier was born on November 18, 1902 outside Ramelton, a small town on the shores of Lough Swilly, in Co. Donegal. All in his family were members of the Second Presbyterian Church in Ramelton.

When he was thirteen years old, he attended Foyle College in the City of Londonderry, and from there he went to Queens University, Belfast where he studied the Classics.

While a student in Belfast he attended Ravenhill Presbyterian Church, and became best friends with the minister's son, Charlie. Charlie would often speak to him about the Lord and of his need of salvation.

Mr. Grier, in referring to his own conversion, made mention of one particular sermon that he heard William Nicholson preach in Rosemary Street Presbyterian Church on October 24, 1922. The sermon was based on John 6:37, "All that the Father giveth me shall come to me: and him that cometh to me I will in no wise cast out." Sometime later he met Charlie Ross in University Avenue and exclaimed to him with joy, "I am the Lord's."

REV. JAMES DUNLOP
Oldpark Presbyterian Church

W. P. Nicholson held a mission in Wellington Street Presbyterian Church, Ballymena, during March and April, 1923, and one night in that mission I had to surrender to Christ. The one who helped me in my decision was an elder and Sabbath school teacher, Mr. Sam Barr. When one refers to those revival years, people invariably think of one's conversion as stirring and catastrophic; mine at least was not. In a quiet place through Mr. Nicholson's ministry, Christ met me, and I yielded. Here is the decision card that I signed in his mission in Ballymena in 1923.

A W. P. NICHOLSON 'DECISION CARD'

My Decision
I take God the Father to be my God. (I Thess. 1:9)
I take God the Son to be my Saviour. (Acts 5:31)
I take God the Holy Ghost to be my Sanctifier. (I Peter 1:2)
I take the Word of God to be my rule. (II Timothy 3:16, 17)
I take the people of God to be my people. (Ruth 1:16, 17)
I likewise dedicate myself wholly to the Lord. (Romans 14:7, 8)
And this I do prayerfully, (Psalm 119:94) deliberately, (Joshua 24:15) sincerely, (II Corinthians 1:12) freely (Psalm 110:3) and for ever. (Romans 8:35-39)

Signed..........................
Dated............................

Not long after, again in my own church, I felt that God wanted me to be in full time service for Him, and from that time, by His grace, that has been my life.

Dr. Dunlop was one of three Nicholson converts who became Moderator of the Irish Presbyterian Church.

JOHN COSTLEY
A Christian Worker

Not all of William' converts made their mark for the Lord as preachers or missionaries, but thousands of them became dedicated Christian workers whose influence was felt in Sunday Schools, Bible Classes, Open Airs and many other avenues of Christian service.

John Costley was a character much loved for his plain speaking and straight-as-a-dye personality. In 1920, at the age of sixteen, he was invited to the Nicholson mission in Ravenhill Presbyterian Church. At that mission a great number of souls responded to the appeals, and among them was young John Costley.

Although John did not become a preacher he lived a dedicated Christian life and was committed to winning the lost for Christ.

On one occasion he organised an evangelistic mission in Keswick Street Mission Hall and invited a young minister by the name of Ian R. K. Paisley (a preacher who quickly became every bit as colourful and controversial as William) to be the evangelist. As a result of that mission over seventy men and women were converted to Christ.

John did not have an easy life. The death of his young wife left him with a broken heart and seven children to care for, but his faith never wavered, and he continued to put the Lord first in his life. He never had much of this world's material possessions, but what he had he shared with all who knew and loved him. His favourite text was Philippians 4:11, "Not that I speak in respect of want: for I have learned, in whatsoever state I am, therewith to be content."

William often said, "Salvation is like the soles of your feet, it wears well." This was certainly true in the life of John Costley.

Chapter Nineteen

HUMOUR IN THE PULPIT

The famous Baptist preacher, Charles Haddon Spurgeon, was once rebuked for introducing humour into his sermons. With a twinkle in his eye he replied, "If only you knew how much I hold back, you would commend me." Defending his use of humour in the pulpit, he wrote, "There are things in these sermons that may produce smiles, but what of them? The preacher is not quite sure about a smile being a sin, and at any rate he thinks it less of a crime to cause a momentary laughter than half an hour of profound slumber."

Like Spurgeon, William knew the value of humour as a tool of evangelism. In justification of his use of humour he said, "Some say you should not make them laugh. But ninety percent of my audiences are babies. If I was to stand solemnly in the pulpit you would say, 'That is dry; it is dead,' so I have to tickle you and keep you in good humour, and all the time you are laughing and feeling good I am jagging at you and getting something down. When a minister gets his nose on the paper to read his sermon, people begin to doze."

With this in mind, I introduce some of the amusing things that William said and did in the pulpit.

At a certain praise service William had six local ministers with him in the pulpit. He asked the congregation, "Have you ever heard your ministers sing? No! Well, you are in for a treat tonight; they are going to sing the next verse by themselves, and we will all join in for the chorus." The embarrassed ministers did their best, and William said, "Wasn't that good!—good for nothing!" Then he thanked them and said, "We will all sing the next verse."

In the Lurgan mission in 1922 William was leading the congregation in the opening hymn of praise, *Jesus the Name High Over All,* when he noticed a man having difficulty finding a seat. He began to read the opening words of the first verse of the hymn, "Jesus the name high over all" when suddenly he called out to an usher, "Find that man a seat." He then continued with the second line of the hymn, "In heaven, earth or hell," which brought roars of laughter throughout the congregation.

Another incident is told concerning his mission in Lurgan. The town clerk, who was a Christian, was completely bald. He also had a bad habit of coming to church late. William did not like latecomers disturbing the meeting. One night when the Presbyterian Church was packed, in came the bald town clerk; he walked into the aisle and looked all around for a seat. William stopped the meeting to shout, "Hi man, it was not combing your hair that kept you late."

A woman came to William once and said, "Sir my husband beats me." He said, "I can easily remedy that. Get him to the service." She said, "I will do my best." He said, 'The night you are in the service and he is with you, give me a nod, and I will know he is there." And sure enough one night the woman was there, and a man was sitting beside her. She gave William a nod, and he nodded back. When it came to the offering, he said, "I have something to say. There is a man in this meeting who beats his wife. What a dirty coward and rascal he is." Then he gave this man, without pointing him out, a terrible dressing down. "Now I am prepared to be generous," he said, "as the plate is passed I will watch what that man gives, and if he does not put on a ten shilling note, I will name him after the offering is lifted." That night the plates were cluttered with ten shilling notes!

Another classic story is told concerning a meeting in Rosemary Street Church. As William was preaching, a drunk man began to disturb the meeting. William told him to shut up, or he would have him thrown out. The man continued to disturb the meeting, so William, as the congregation was singing, left the pulpit, walked down the aisle, caught him by the scruff of the neck, opened the church door and threw him into the middle of Rosemary Street. He slammed the door, and as he was walking back up the aisle someone said to him, "Mr. Nicholson, the Saviour would not have done that." "No," said William, "the Saviour would have cast the devil out of the man; I cannot do that, so I did the next best thing—I cast them both out."

A cigarette smoker told William that smoking was his only comfort in life. William's reply was typical: "Jesus has said, 'I will not leave you comfortless,' and I have never thought that statement to mean tobacco, but it is well to know Scripture a little better every day one lives." "I don't mean that," said the smoker. William replied, "Nor do I, you dirty old chimney pot. If the Lord had intended you to smoke, He would have turned you upside down, and every time you would have sneezed, you would have blown your hat off! Half-baked, that is what you are!"

One night at a prayer meeting, William asked a friend called Bob from Bangor to pray. Bob had never prayed in public before, but he obeyed. Remembering that William had a lot to say about the devil, he thought it would be appropriate to bring him into his prayer. "Lord, don't let the devil get a victory tonight," he prayed. "Yes Lord, tie a knot in his tail," interjected William. That was the end of Bob's prayer.

In another prayer meeting a brother, who had a very high pitched voice prayed. When he had finished, William shouted out, "God bless you, brother, only a mother could love you with a voice like that!"

William preached powerfully upon honesty and the repaying of debts. In one service he said, "If all the clothes that some of you are wearing and haven't paid for were to drop off, I would have to ask the ushers to put out the lights'.

Throughout his ministry, William had a long and warm association with the Christian Workers Union. One afternoon during a tent mission held in Church Meadow, Ballynahinch, a car drove into the meadow. An elderly lady, who had never heard William and who was anxious to meet him, thought (although mistakenly) that there was an afternoon meeting on that day and asked someone to take her to it in his car. When she discovered her mistake, she decided to wait for the evening meeting. Someone gave her tea, and later on, she was seated among the crowd when William mounted the platform.

The meeting went on, and he began to preach. Suddenly, in the middle of the sermon, a car was heard being started outside. The old lady thought it was the car in which she had come; she thought it was going to leave without her. She realised that she would have to leave immediately. But before she left she wanted just to shake hands with William.

Most people who have interrupted William during a sermon have had cause to regret it, but he was surprisingly gentle with this old lady. When she came near him, he seemed at a loss to know what to do, but he accepted her proffered hand and shook it. "Good-bye, Granny," he said, "I'll meet you in heaven."

She appeared to be doubtful about that. "Well," she said, and she paused a good while, "I hope—I hope you'll be there."

On one occasion in a meeting in 'Ahoghill Cathedral' a young lady came in wearing a very bright yellow dress. The place was absolutely packed, and two elderly women in the front row were spread along the seat. The young girl could not get a seat. William smiled as he looked down at the two women in the front seat and said, "If you two clucking hens would pull in your wings, that canary could get in beside you."

Chapter Twenty

HOOKS

preacher once said, "An apt illustration sticks in the soul like a hook in a fish's mouth."

As a fisher of men, William was masterful in his use of illustrations, and they proved effective hooks in fishing for souls. The following are a few that helped make vital points come alive.

THE MOODY CHURCH

I remember preaching in Moody's church in Chicago—in the old church yonder at the corner. Over the platform or pulpit Mr Moody used to have the words "God is love" brightly lighted up by electric light or gas light. These lights were burning all the time he was preaching. One Sunday night a burglar, who was going to do a job, came along. He peeked in through the church door, then he opened the door and looked in. He saw the words "God is love." He shut the door and went down the steps cursing and swearing. The farther he walked along the street the hotter he became, and the madder he became the more he cursed and damned. He said, "God is not love. I have been kicked and cursed since ever I was born. I never had a chance. Everything is against me. God is against me. It is not true; it is a lie. God doesn't love me."

But the farther he walked the more he was troubled, and it was not too long till he turned back towards the church. When he got to the door of the church Mr. Moody was giving an invitation to his hearers to come to Christ. This burglar walked right down the aisle, fell at the altar, and accepted Jesus Christ as Saviour.

You may be cast out by everybody; you may be down and out tonight; you may feel heart-broken; you may feel as lonely as a man or a woman can be in a big city—and man, I know what that is—as if everybody had turned on you, and you think your life is hardly worth living. On the other hand, you may be as respectable as man or a woman can be, with all your white-washed hypocrisy and religiosity and profession; it doesn't matter whether you are up and out or down and out; thank God, He loves you. Shouldn't that be an encouragement to you to come to Christ? He is willing to receive you—"He loved me, and gave Himself for me."

MADAME TUSSAUDS

I remember that on one occasion I was up in London, and I went to Madame Tussaud's to see the waxworks. When I entered the premises I went up to a woman to put my couple of bob down. It was a wax figure of a woman! I looked around to see if anybody was watching the greenhorn, and I said to myself. "I won't be taken in this time," so I marched past the next woman who was sitting in the place to take money. I thought that it was a wax figure, too! But there was a big policeman on the other side, and I thought he was a wax figure. Said I, "You can't take me in this time," and I marched through. The big policeman "nabbed" me. He said, "Where's your couple of bob?" I gave in; I didn't try to be wise any more! The wax figure had a name: dead. Presbyterian, Methodist, Baptist, Plymouth Brother, Christian: A name to live: dead.

Do you know anybody like that—a Christless Christian, a name to live and dead? Paul speaks of them as lovers of pleasure more than lovers of God. They are quite at home in a picture show, but in a prayer meeting they are like old hens in a duckpond! Man alive, they enjoy themselves in the world and in the pleasures of it, but in the things of God and the means of grace—they are stones instead of bread to them, scorpions instead of fish.

CHARLOTTE ELLIOTT

Charlotte Elliott had been brought into the fellowship of the Church at Easter time. Her godly minister thought she was truly converted and that her soul rested on Christ. One day he was going past where she lived, and she was coming out of her house dressed for a ball and stepped into a carriage. The old man nearly dropped on seeing that, and he went quickly before the carriage door was closed, and said, "Charlotte, are you saved?" She banged the door closed and got away from the old man, but she did not get away from his question. Instead of dancing till daylight, she was home before midnight, and for a long week her pride was dying. At last she could stand it no more, and she started to seek the minister. As she was making her way to where he lived, she met him on the street, and she said, "I'm delighted to see you. I was making my way to your home, and I have come for two things. First, I apologise to you for my rudeness." "That's all right, Charlotte; I understand it." "Sir, how am I to answer that question you asked me?" "Charlotte," he said, "just as you are, come to Christ." Just as she was she came to Christ, and some time afterwards she wrote these beautiful words which have been the means of leading thousands to Him:

Just as I am without one plea,
But that Thy blood was shed for me,
And that Thou bids't me come to Thee,
O Lamb of God, I come.

Just as I am and waiting not
To rid my soul of one dark blot,
To Thee, Whose blood can cleanse each spot,
O Lamb of God, I come.

That is the way you have got to come, that is the way we have all got to come, and you may come right now, just as you are, for "Him that cometh to Me, I will in no wise cast out."

READING THE BIBLE

A father wondered how he could best entertain his children and yet allow himself freedom to read his paper. He bought a box of blocks with the map of Great Britain on them. He thought this would keep them busy and quiet and let him read his paper. He had hardly settled down to read until they shouted, "We have done it." He was surprised and looked around, and sure enough, the map was complete. He said, "You surely have learned your geography well." The youngest child said, "You see, Father, there is a picture of a man on the other side, so when we got the man right, the map was right." So it is when reading the Bible, when we get the Man in His rightful place in the Bible, then the Bible becomes a divine unity without mistake or error.

GOD'S UNSPEAKABLE GIFT

A little fellow was sitting by the side of his mother as she lay dying on a heap of rags in a room in the slums of London. She said she wished she could taste a grape and ease her parched tongue. A short time previously the little lad had been taken to Buckingham Palace by his Sunday School on its annual outing. While there they were shown through the beautiful conservatories, and they saw the vines loaded with luscious bunches of grapes. As the wee fellow listened to his dying mother's wish, he remembered those beautiful grapes, and said, "Don't worry, mother; I'll get you some grapes." So off he started, and arrived at the gates of the Palace. The sentinels laughed at the wee ragged boy when they heard his request. But he started weeping and wondering. Just then King Edward drove in, and seeing the poor boy, he ordered the carriage to be stopped and the boy to be brought to him. When the boy was brought, the King asked him what his trouble was. The boy told him his mother was dying and wished she could taste a grape, and as he had seen so many here the other day at the Sunday School outing, he thought he would come and ask for some. The King at once ordered a bunch to be brought, and handed it to the wee ragged urchin, saying that he hoped they would help his mother. The wee fellow, not knowing it was the King, stood before him with his ragged cap in his hand and thanked him, and then pulling out a halfpenny offered it to the King and said, "Sir, it is all I have." Tears filled the King's eyes, and he said, "My boy, the King doesn't sell his grapes; he freely gives them." How many are doing the same to Jesus about eternal life? They know they cannot buy eternal life, but they would like to give something for it—however poor and small it may be. A good life or regular attendance at the church or generosity—something or other, however small. It will help them to feel better. They won't feel as if they were poor bankrupts. Their pride would be gratified. Friend! it is God's Unspeakable Gift, and can never be merited or purchased. Receive it freely, and receive it now!

GOD'S HAND UPON YOU

I fear to let you go. I feel like the nurse in a hospital during the Civil War. A young lad had his arm and shoulder fearfully shattered by a shell. They did their best for him, but the limb and body were so shattered that they could not very securely tie up the arteries. The nurse was given orders to see that the wounded lad was not allowed to move. The nurse sat by his side as he moaned and talked in his delirium. Toward morning he quietened down. One of the other patients demanded her services, and she thought, as the lad was so quiet, she could leave him and attend to the others.

When she returned she discovered to her horror that the lad had moved, and the blood was oozing through the bandages and bed and onto the floor. She stripped of the bandages, and seizing the artery, sent for the physician. When he came he said she might as well let go, as he must die. Nothing could be done. The bleeding had brought the lad to consciousness, and he heard the doctor's words of doom. Looking up into the nurse's face, he pleaded with her not to let go, as he was unfit and unready to die. He had run away from mother and home. She turned away her head, and when she looked again he had gone into eternity. God has placed you under my hand today. You are conscious of your danger. I have my hand still upon you. Will you not decide? Oh, I pray you, do not delay. I cannot hold you much longer. I pray God that my letting you go now may not mean your death and damnation.

RECONCILIATION

In the North of England there was a family—one of the most respectable and respected families and one of the oldest families in the country. They had only one boy, and when he grew up to years of responsibility he developed habits of gambling and drinking, His father was a Christian man and a Member of Parliament for that district. This son, by his drunken habits, brought his name to shame and disgrace. His father had again and again redeemed him, paid his debts and got him out of trouble; but at last, broken-hearted, he said, "John, if you stop this life and live as you ought to live, this home is yours. But if you intend to live as you have been living, I have paid your debts for the last time. There is the door." And the young fellow picked up his hat and left the home. A father is not like a mother, and although the father grew impatient, the mother's love was never exhausted. She became sad hearted and faded away, and in spite of all that was done to lift her spirits, she sank into decline. They took her to physician after physician and from health resort to health resort, and after years of trouble and expense she came home to die.

The doctor said, "Madam, I fear you will pass away today." And when the doctor came out the husband said, "Well?" And the doctor said, "This is her last day here." The husband went to his wife's bedside. She was lying there white and weak, and with her emaciated hands she took his and said, "You know what is bringing me to a premature grave. I am dying, and would like to look into the face of my child once more. Oh, grant me this dying request. My heart is hungry, withered and broken; but now it is the end. John, I will never have another petition to ask; but I would like to see my boy before I die. It would ease my deathbed and make it bright."

They discovered the boy was in Newcastle-on-Tyne, and they wired him. He got the wire, and with a broken heart he read the message. I have sat many a time sat yonder in the Salvation Army barracks at Mafeking, South Africa, with the tears running down my cheeks. Though we would not listen to the preaching, we used to listen to the singing, and there was one woman who used to sing:

> *Your mother still prays for you, Jack,*
> *Your mother still prays for you, Jack,*
> *In that land far away o'er the ocean,*
> *Your mother still prays for you.*

I have seen three hundred of us sitting there sobbing; we all had good mothers. When this young fellow got the wire telling him his mother was dying, it seemed as if the trains were too slow; and when he came to the door he did not knock, he did not need to ask which was her room. In that bedroom he had seen the light of the world. There he had learned to pray. Once he was fair as the morning dew as he knelt at his mother's knee. But now, sin stained and marred, he came home. Kneeling down, he began, "Oh, mother, my sin has broken your heart and is bringing you to a premature grave. My God, to think that I am the murderer of my mother! Is there forgiveness with you or with God?" And she said, "John, I have never ceased to love you. While it is true your sin and conduct have broken my heart, it is also true that my love has followed you all the years; and John, if your mother never ceases to love you, what must God be like towards you? Oh John, I am dying, but it seems to me I will have to tell Jesus my heaven will be no heaven if you do not come there. Will you promise me, my boy, that you will meet me yonder, that you will take Christ as your Saviour tonight and then meet mother in the realms of glory?" "Yes, mother, by the grace of God, I will follow Christ." And she turned to her husband and said, "John, our life has been happy. God has given us this child. and now I will make another request. I want you to be reconciled to Him. He has given himself to Christ, and by God's grace will never bring shame on your name again. Will you not be reconciled to your boy?"

She raised herself in her bed, and taking her husband's hand in hers, and her son's hand in the other, she brought the two together in a clasp, and then fell back on her pillow a lifeless corpse. The two men, grasping each other's hands, looked into each other's eyes and then into the face of the mother and wife, and with the tears blinding their eyes they were reconciled over the dead mother.

Men, today will you be reconciled to God over the broken body of Jesus? He puts His nail pierced hand out to you, and He says, "Oh, be ye reconciled to God." Will you put your hand in His and obtain mercy? God help you!

Chapter Twenty-One

THE LAST VOYAGE

For over sixty years William travelled the world preaching the Gospel. Like John Wesley, he could say, "The world is my parish." His travels brought him to New Zealand, Australia, South Africa, America and the British Isles.

He and Mrs. Nicholson revisited the North of Ireland on several occasions between the late summer of 1928 and 1958. In 1958, in spite of doctor's warnings, he held a number of what he called Kangaroo Missions, throughout the country.

Reports of the missions which took place in Lisburn and Londonderry, spoke of the crowds being so great, that the meetings always commenced half an hour before the advertised time.

On the opening night of the mission in Londonderry, William prefaced his address by saying, "I never thought I would see Ireland again. I have been told by my doctors that my days are numbered and my preaching days are over. When I was invited back to Ulster, I was a bit hesitant, but when I mentioned the matter to my wife, the bags were packed, and off we started again.

"I think," he said wistfully, "that this is the last time, unless the Lord makes me a centurion."

He was not long "on the bridge" until all the well known features of a Nicholson meeting were in evidence. Once he took command of the service, he soon had the congregation singing heartily the same familiar choruses, and he showed his love for the unusual by having the men and women whistling in turn.

His preaching was still as fearless and uncompromising as it had been in the revival days of the early twenties. Hypocrisy was exposed with holy boldness, and his passion for godly living among believers was matched by his love for the lost.

His campaign ended in November, and at his farewell meeting in the Wellington Hall in Belfast, he related how he had said in one of his meetings that he was an octogenarian. A little girl who was present asked her mother, "Mother, what is an octogenarian?" Her mother told her to look up the meaning in a dictionary when she got home. Later the little girl came back to her mother with the news that she now knew what Mr. Nicholson meant. "He is an octopus," she said. This raised a chorus of laughter throughout the congregation.

He spoke on the subject "A Double Portion," and he took his text from II Kings 2:9. The meeting ended with the Nicholson Doxology— *Down in the Dumps I'll Never Go*, and everyone waved their handkerchiefs as they sang *God Be With You Till We Meet Again*.

William and his wife returned to their home in Glendale, California, and unfortunately his health continued to decline.

In the autumn of 1959 arrangements were made for them to return to Ireland so that they could spend their remaining days at the Bangor home of his brother-in-law, Dr. J. B. Hanna. While making the trans-Atlantic journey on board the Mauritania, he suffered a very serious heart attack and was so ill that the doctor decided to have him brought ashore at the first port of call which was Cork in the Republic of Ireland.

He was immediately taken to the Victoria Hospital where his condition continued to deteriorate.

Two weeks later, on Thursday, October 29, at the age of eighty-three, William Patteson Nicholson entered into the immediate presence of his Lord and Master.

The funeral took place at the Hamilton Road Presbyterian Church, Bangor, on Monday, November 2, at two in the afternoon. A company of over one thousand people—ministers and laymen and missionaries and evangelists all gathered to pay their last tribute to a faithful and fearless evangelist who had been an instrument through whom blessing had flowed to many. He had now finished his course and had entered into his eternal reward.

The service in the church was conducted by Rev. David Burke who opened with the 23rd Psalm and a prayer. The second hymn was John Newton's *How Sweet the Name of Jesus Sounds* after which Mr. Noel Grant read the Scriptures.

After the singing of William Cowper's hymn *There is a Fountain Filled With Blood* the Rev. James Dunlop gave the address in the form of a tribute.

In many places over the world, in spheres high and low, he became a blessing to his fellowmen; and we here in his native Ulster are not likely for a long time to forget how mightily God chose to work through him in the early 1920's especially. We all know that he became in some respects a controversial figure; often times, in his zeal, he brought not peace on the earth, but a sword, like his Lord; but none could deny his passion for the Gospel nor the power with which he presented it to men. I have never known such a preacher of the Gospel as the Rev. W. P. Nicholson; I have never known one who, under God, made such an appeal to men particularly, in their own language. Here was one whom God was pleased to raise up at a critical time in the history of our Province to call people from sin and civil strife to repentance and faith towards Jesus Christ, one who, in a remarkable degree, was given the ear of the people, and one who was the instrument of leading hundreds of individuals into a vital, regenerating experience of God's grace in Christ so that their lives were transformed. And that movement of God and its impetus on the work of God in this and other lands remain to this day.

Our praise at this service is not to the man but to the power of God in and through him. As he now stands before the Throne in his Lord's presence, we would re-echo the cry, "Not unto us, not unto us, O Lord, but unto Thy Name be glory!" His earthly motto was, "He must increase, and I must decrease," and now "the Lamb must have all the glory in Emmanuel's land." But we give thanks for him, and we feel the constraint of his unfaltering devotion to spend our strength and wear out our days in the service of the same Lord and Saviour, which is the one thing that matters in the last resort.

He is gone from us, yet, just a little before us. But he is not dead; he is alive. The trumpets have sounded for him on the other side. And what a host have greeted and will greet him over there, to whom, as to so many of us here, he was the very savour of life! The triumphant Christian assurance, which he reiterated again and again, of the life beyond with Christ, which is far better, is now a reality to him, and, behold, the half had not been told.

So we take leave of W. P. Nicholson until the morning, and as we think of his influence on earth in his time and consider the times in which we now live, we are constrained to cry:

God give us men! A time like this demands
Strong men, great hearts, true faith and ready hands.
Men whom the lust of office does not kill,
Men whom the spoils of office cannot buy,
Men who possess opinions and a will,
Men who have honour—men who will not lie,
Men who can stand before a demagogue and
Storm his treacherous flatteries without winking;
Tall men! Sun-crowned, who live above the fog
In public duty, and in private thinking.
God give us men!

The Rev. John T. Carson, himself a Nicholson convert, offered a thanksgiving prayer for the life and ministry of William, and the service was concluded with the singing of the triumphant hymn *For All the Saints, Who From Their Labours Rest.*

A large company then made their way to the new Clandeboye Cemetery for the service at the graveside. The Rev. Burke began the service with the much loved hymn There is a Fountain Filled With Blood after which Mr. R. Fraser read the Scriptures. The Rev. James Wisheart, gave a short address in which he said he wished to pay the tribute of a son in the faith to Mr. Nicholson. He was brought to a knowledge of Jesus Christ as Saviour on the September 21, 1922, in the mission held in The Cripples Institute, Donegall Road. Little did he think then that he would enter the Christian ministry, or that he would be asked to pay tribute to the life and memory of W. P. Nicholson.

After the committal by the Rev. John Carson, prayer was offered by Pastor W. Weir and by Mr. W. Wylie.

His gravestone records the date of his birth and also the date of his rebirth:

In
Loving Memory of
Rev. William Patteson Nicholson
Beloved Husband of F. Elizabeth Nicholson
Born 3rd April 1876 - Born again 22nd May 1889
Called Home 29th October 1959
John 10:41-42: John did no miracle: but all things
that John spake of this man (Jesus) were true
and many believed on him there.

No truer eulogy could be pronounced on William than that which had been expressed by Regent Morton when the earthly remains of the Scottish Reformer, John Knox, were laid to rest in St. Giles' Church-yard, Edinburgh: "There lies he who never feared the face of man."

What does the life and ministry of William Patteson Nicholson have to say to us as we pray for revival in our own day and generation? The question must be asked, "What can we learn from the life and ministry of W. P. Nicholson?" Let us consider some of the answers to that important question.

God is sovereign in His choice of instrument to bring revival. We are often amazed at God's chosen instruments. William was an earthern vessel, his language at times ungracious. He was abusive to those who would criticise him or who interrupted his meetings by their late arrival. But in spite of all that, God in His sovereignty was pleased to use him for the furtherance of the Gospel and revival of His Church.

The importance of the Spirit's blessing. William could say "the Spirit of the Lord is upon me because He hath anointed me to preach the Gospel." He was convinced that his success as an evangelist could be dated to that moment in his life when he surrendered fully, laid all on the altar of sacrifice and received by faith the gift of the Holy Spirit. Before he began to preach, William would often pray:

> I take the promised Holy Ghost,
> I take the gift of Pentecost,
> To fill me to the uttermost,
> I take—He undertakes.

The power of prayer and the ability of God to fulfill the promises contained in His Word. William often expressed his gratitude that he had been given a "believing mind." His life was one of dependance upon the faithfulness of God to fulfill His promises. A frequent saying of his was "If you worry you do not trust, and if you trust you do not worry." One of his favourite texts was John 14:13-14, "And whatsoever ye shall ask in my name, that will I do, that the Father may be glorified in the Son. If ye shall ask any thing in my name, I will do it." When preaching on the problem of prayer, he said, "These words of our Lord Jesus are as true for us today as they were for the disciples long ago. The Lord can as truly fulfil them for us today as He did for them. Don't let us dodge or evade them or change them; let us face them openly and honestly and put them to the test, and give Him a chance to show to the world that "He keepeth His promises for ever.   Hallelujah!"

A burden for the lost. William was a man with a vision and a burden for lost souls. He prayed, "O for a passionate passion for souls—a heart to feel so deeply that we would rather not live than live and get no souls saved."

He did not believe that soul-winning was just for evangelists. He said, "The work of witnessing is the duty of the whole church; the field of witnessing is the territory of the whole world, and the power of witnessing is a personal Pentecost."

William believed that it was the responsibility of every Christian to proclaim the good news of the Gospel to all men with that same consuming passion.

Proclaim God's Word with boldness. William could say with Paul, "For if the trumpet give an uncertain sound, who shall prepare himself to the battle?" (I Corinthians 14:8) He made sure his message was not muted or misunderstood. He preached in the language of the farm labourer and the shipyard worker. His was the vocabulary of the street. No-one needed a dictionary to understand his message. In the first nights of his missions William usually preached to the Christians, exposing the sins of pride, hypocrisy, prayerlessness, worldliness and defective consecration. He insisted upon Christians putting things right with one another and making restitution whenever possible. He had no time for half-baked believers. He was fully committed to the authority and infallibility of the Word of God. At a time when the poison of modernism was making inroads, he spoke out faithfully and fervently in defence of the Scriptures of truth. George Whitefield wrote, "I love those that thunder out the Word. The Christian world is in a deep sleep. Nothing but a loud voice can awaken them out of it." Truly Whitefield would have approved of William Patteson Nicholson's trumpet tones.

Perhaps supremely we learn to be zealous for the Lord's glory. His life's motto was "He must increase, and I must decrease." In everything he said and did his desire was that the Lord would be glorified. He could say at the end of a life which was lived on the altar of dedication, "Father I have glorified Thee on earth; I have finished the work Thou gavest me to do."

William Patteson Nicholson became God's mouthpiece to his generation. There are multitudes of men and women throughout the world today who thank God for His honoured instrument. Oh for a prophet for our day, armed with the same truth and empowered by the same Spirit to see another, and greater revival to the glory of God!

ACKNOWLEDGEMENTS

Mr. S. W. Murray author of W. P. Nicholson - Flame for God and Ulster, for the use of some of his unpublished material and for his constant encouragement in writing this book.

Mr. Ian Kinnaird of Cottown, for the use of family photographs.

Mr. Tom Knutson who edited the final manuscript.

Mr. Samuel Lowry of Ambassador Productions Ltd. for entrusting me with the task of writing this biography.